Taste of Home's

Fast Fixes
with Mixes

Taste of Home

A TASTE OF HOME/READER'S DIGEST BOOK

© 2006 Reiman Media Group, Inc.
5400 S. 60th St., Greendale WI 53129
All rights reserved.

Taste of Home and Reader's Digest are registered trademarks
of The Reader's Digest Association, Inc.

Editor: Kathy Pohl
Project Editor: Cheryl Winters-Tetreau
Project Designer: Sandy Freeman
Cover Designer: Emma Acevedo
Proofreader: Jean Steiner
Editorial Assistant: Barb Czysz
Recipe Testing and Editing: Taste of Home Test Kitchen
Food Photography: Reiman Photo Studio

Executive Editor/Books: Heidi Reuter Lloyd
Senior Editor/Retail Books: Jennifer Olski
Creative Director: Ardyth Cope
Senior Vice President/Editor in Chief: Catherine Cassidy
President: Barbara Newton
Founder: Roy Reiman

Pictured on front cover: Chocolate Praline Torte, page 182
Left to right: Lasagna Soup, page 111; Sweet and Sour Meat Loaf, page 82;
Garlic Potatoes and Ham, page 87; Kool-Aid Floats, page 14.
Pictured on back cover: Pork Chops with Apples and Stuffing, page 61;
Herb Tossed Salad, page 35.
Cover photo by: Jim Wieland

International Standard Book Number (10): 0-89821-469-6
International Standard Book Number (13): 978-0-89821-469-7
Library of Congress Control Number: 2006925316

For other Taste of Home books and products, visit www.tasteofhome.com.
For more Reader's Digest products and information, visit
www.rd.com (in the United States)
www.rd.ca (in Canada)

Printed in China.
3 5 7 9 10 8 6 4

Contents

INTRODUCTION

 With the hectic schedules so many families have these days, it's not easy to serve a sit-down meal night after night. But with the help of prepared mixes, you can whip up a homestyle dinner—or breakfast, lunch, or dessert—in a flash. What's the secret? Savory recipes from simple mixes that cut prep time without sacrificing taste!

Here you'll discover shortcut recipes developed by the readers of *Taste of Home*, the No. 1 cooking magazine in the country, and the Taste of Home Test Kitchen. Start with a soup mix, pudding mix or cake mix, add a few everyday items from your refrigerator or pantry, and you'll see how easy it is cut down on your time in the kitchen and still serve delicious meals that will have your family asking for more.

In the mood for chicken? Check out our Quicker Chicken and Dumplings on page 51. It goes from prep to table in 20 minutes! Or maybe your family is hankering for something spicy—if so, serve them Fiesta Fry Pan Dinner on page 73. Is there a beef lover in the family? Then Beef Veggie Casserole on page 80 is sure to please. By using gravy mix, frozen vegetables and refrigerated biscuits, you can serve a hearty stew in under 30 minutes.

When the weather turns cold, every-one looks forward to a bowl of hot, steamy homemade soup—but who has the time to make it? You do, when you use one of our many soup recipes in Chapter 5. Take Wild Rice Soup (page 108) for example. All you'll need is chicken broth, condensed soup and a rice mix, and you'll have a pot of savory soup in a fraction of the time it would take to make it all from scratch. Or try our flavorful Lasagna Soup on page 111. Packaged lasagna dinner mix, along with canned tomatoes and corn, speed up the time from stove to table.

Of course, no dinner is complete without a sumptuous dessert. And now you can surprise family and friends with tempting treats they'll think you spent *hours* preparing. Only you'll know the secret—timesaving recipes that use mixes to get the job done! You'll find two chapters packed with quick and easy dessert choices: Cakes, Cookies & Bars and More Sweet Treats. The recipe for Quick Little Devils, on page136, has only four ingredients—devil's food cake mix, butter, marshmallow creme and peanut butter—but yields chocolaty peanut butter squares that are sure to satisfy any sweet tooth.

With *Taste of Home's Fast Fixes with Mixes,* you won't have to resort to a dash through the drive-thru. It's never been easier to put fast and fabulous food on the table in a flash!

—The Editors

CHAPTER 1

Snacks & Beverages

Turkey Taco Dip

1 pound ground turkey breast
1 envelope reduced-sodium taco seasoning
1 cup water
1 package (8 ounces) fat-free cream cheese, softened
1 cup (8 ounces) fat-free sour cream
¾ cup picante sauce
½ cup shredded lettuce
1 cup chopped fresh tomato
1 cup (4 ounces) shredded fat-free cheddar cheese
Baked tortilla chips

In a skillet, cook turkey over medium heat until no longer pink; drain. Add taco seasoning and water; cover and simmer for 10 minutes. Spoon turkey onto a 12-in. serving plate or pizza pan. In a mixing bowl, beat the cream cheese until smooth. Add sour cream; spread over the meat mixture. Spread with picante sauce. Top with lettuce, tomato and cheese. Serve with tortilla chips. **Yield:** 10 servings.

Monster Munchies

Magically transform squash or pumpkin seeds into this spell-binding snack from the Taste of Home Test Kitchen.

1 cup seeds from freshly cut squash *or* pumpkin, washed and dried
2 tablespoons vegetable oil
1–2 tablespoons ranch salad dressing mix

In a skillet, saute seeds in oil for 5 minutes or until lightly browned. Using a slotted spoon, transfer seeds to an ungreased 15-in. × 10-in. × 1-in. baking pan. Sprinkle with salad dressing mix; stir to coat. Spread in a single layer. Bake at 325° for 10–15 minutes or until crisp. Store in an airtight container for up to 3 weeks. **Yield:** 1 cup.

Mushroom Spinach Dip

This thick, creamy mixture from the Taste of Home Test Kitchen gets its fresh flavor from mushrooms, spinach and green onions. Serve it in a bowl with a platter of crackers or crunchy vegetables.

1 package (10 ounces) frozen chopped spinach, thawed and squeezed dry
1½ cups (12 ounces) sour cream
1 cup mayonnaise
1 package vegetable soup mix
1 cup chopped fresh mushrooms
3 green onions, finely chopped
Raw vegetables *or* crackers

In a bowl, combine the spinach, sour cream, mayonnaise, soup mix, mushrooms and onions; mix well. Cover and refrigerate for 2 hours. Serve with vegetables or crackers. **Yield:** 3 cups.

Cucumber Sandwiches

"I was introduced to a similar sandwich by a friend many years ago," recalls Karen Schriefer of Stevensville, Maryland. *"I sometimes add thinly sliced onions for a change of pace."*

1 carton (8 ounces) cream cheese spread
2 teaspoons ranch salad dressing mix
12 slices pumpernickel rye bread
2–3 medium cucumbers

In a bowl, combine cream cheese and dressing mix. Spread on one side of each slice of bread. Peel cucumbers if desired; thinly slice and place on six slices of bread. Top with remaining bread. Serve immediately. **Yield:** 6 servings.

Taco Pickup Sticks

Looking for something a bit different to munch on? Try this zesty snack mix from Kathy Hunt of Dallas, Texas. "We enjoy the extra kick our taste buds get from the spices," she notes. "One batch is never enough to satisfy my crew."

3 cans (7 ounces *each*) potato sticks
2 cans (6 ounces *each*) french-fried onions
1 can (12 ounces) salted peanuts
⅓ cup butter, melted
1 envelope taco seasoning

In a large bowl, combine potato sticks, onions and peanuts. Combine butter and taco seasoning; mix well. Pour over potato stick mixture and toss to coat. Place in three ungreased 15-in. × 10-in. × 1-in. baking pans. Bake, uncovered, at 250° for 45 minutes, stirring every 15 minutes. Store in airtight containers. **Yield:** 24 cups.

Ranch Pretzels

"For a fast, fun snack, start with plain pretzels and add a new taste twist," suggests Lois Kerns of Hagerstown, Maryland. "It takes just a few minutes to coat them with seasonings and pop them into the oven to bake."

1 package (20 ounces) large thick pretzels
1 envelope ranch salad dressing mix
¾ cup vegetable oil
1½ teaspoons dill weed
1½ teaspoons garlic powder

Break pretzels into bite-size pieces and place in a large bowl. Combine remaining ingredients; pour over pretzels. Stir to coat. Pour into an ungreased 15-in. × 10-in. × 1-in. baking pan. Bake at 200° for 1 hour, stirring every 15 minutes. **Yield:** 12 cups.

No-Bake Party Mix

This munchable snack mixture from Regina Stock of Topeka, Kansas is sure to disappear in a hurry at picnics and parties. A packet of ranch salad dressing mix makes it a breeze to throw together.

8 cups Crispix cereal
2½ cups miniature pretzels *or* pretzel sticks
2½ cups bite-size cheddar cheese crackers
3 tablespoons vegetable oil
1 envelope ranch salad dressing mix

In a heavy-duty resealable 2-gal. plastic bag, combine the cereal, pretzels and crackers; drizzle with oil. Seal and toss gently to mix. Sprinkle with dressing mix; seal and toss until well coated. Store in an airtight container. **Yield:** about 12 cups.

Ricotta Pepperoni Dip

From Orange Park, Florida, Barbara Carlucci shares this warm appetizer dip that gets its flavor from an herb soup mix. Crispy golden pizza dough strips are perfect for digging into the thick, cheesy mixture.

PIZZA STICKS:
- 1 tube (10 ounces) refrigerated pizza crust
- 1 tablespoon olive oil
- 2 tablespoons grated Parmesan cheese
- 1 tablespoon Italian seasoning
- ¼ teaspoon garlic powder
- ⅛ teaspoon pepper

DIP:
- 1 cup (8 ounces) sour cream
- 1 cup ricotta cheese
- 1 tablespoon savory herb with garlic soup mix
- ¼ cup chopped pepperoni
- 1 cup (4 ounces) shredded mozzarella cheese
- 1 tablespoon grated Parmesan cheese

On a lightly floured surface, roll out pizza crust to a 12-in. × 8-in. rectangle. Brush with oil. Combine the Parmesan cheese, Italian seasoning, garlic powder and pepper; sprinkle over dough. Cut into 3-in. × 1-in. strips; place on a greased baking sheet. Bake at 425° for 6–9 minutes or until golden brown.

Meanwhile, combine the sour cream, ricotta, soup mix and pepperoni in a saucepan; heat through. Stir in mozzarella and Parmesan cheeses just until melted. Serve warm with pizza sticks. **Yield:** about 2½ dozen pizza sticks and 2 cups dip.

Coconut Fruit Dip

From Lakeville, Massachusetts, Nancy Tanguay shares this fruit dip that has a fun pineapple and coconut flavor. "I usually serve it with melon slices, straw-berries and grapes, but you could use whatever fruit you have on hand. It's a big hit whenever I make it."

1 can (8 ounces) crushed unsweetened pineapple, undrained
¾ cup fat-free milk
½ cup (4 ounces) fat-free sour cream
1 package (3.4 ounces) instant coconut cream pudding mix
Fresh pineapple, grapes and strawberries *or* other fruit

In a blender, combine the first four ingredients; cover and process for 1 minute or until smooth. Serve with fruit. Store in the refrigerator. **Yield:** 2 cups.

Nacho Rice Dip

Spanish rice mix adds an interesting twist to this effortless appetizer from Audra Hungate of Holt, Missouri. "Every time I serve this dip at get-togethers, my guests gobble it up," she writes.

1 package (6.8 ounces) Spanish rice and vermicelli mix
2 tablespoons butter
2 cups water
1 can (14½ ounces) diced tomatoes, undrained
1 pound ground beef
1 pound (16 ounces) process American cheese, cubed
1 can (14½ ounces) stewed tomatoes
1 jar (8 ounces) process cheese sauce
Tortilla chips

In a large saucepan, cook rice mix in butter until golden. Stir in water and diced tomatoes; bring to a boil. Reduce heat; cover and simmer for 15–20 minutes or until rice is tender. Meanwhile, in a skillet, cook beef until no longer pink. Drain and add to the rice. Stir in cheese, stewed tomatoes and cheese sauce; cook and stir until cheese is melted. Transfer to a slow cooker; cover and keep warm on low. Serve with tortilla chips. **Yield:** about 8 cups.

Lemon Ice Tea Mix

"A friend who has a large family and does a lot of entertaining created this mix," explains Linda Fox of Soldotna, Alaska. "It's inexpensive and makes a tasty, refreshing batch of tea."

7½ cups sugar
2 cups unsweetened instant tea
5 envelopes (.23 ounce *each*) unsweetened lemonade drink mix

ADDITIONAL INGREDIENTS:
1 cup warm water
Cold water

Combine sugar, tea and drink mix. Store in an airtight container in a cool, dry place. **Yield:** 5 batches (8½ cups total). **To prepare tea:** Dissolve about 1⅔ cups tea mix in 1 cup warm water. Place in a gallon container. Add cold water to measure 1 gallon. Cover and refrigerate. **Yield:** about 16 (1-cup) servings per batch.

Lemon-Berry Pitcher Punch

"If you need to satisfy a large group, you can double or triple the recipe for this refreshing beverage," advises Margaret O'Bryon from Bel Air, Maryland. The tangy combination of lemonade and cranberry juice is a real thirst-quencher on a warm day.

½ cup sweetened lemonade drink mix
4 cups cold water
⅔ cup cranberry juice, chilled
1½ cups lemon-lime soda, chilled

In a pitcher, combine drink mix, water and cranberry juice. Stir in soda. Serve immediately. **Yield:** about 6 cups.

Friendship Tea Mix

Arma White combines seven simple ingredients to make a big batch of this hot spiced drink mix. "Placed in a jar and tied with pretty ribbon, this is one of my favorite gifts for neighbors," reports the Golconda, Illinois cook.

1 jar (21.1 ounces) **orange breakfast drink mix**
1 cup **sugar**
½ cup **sweetened lemonade drink mix**
½ cup **unsweetened instant tea**
1 package (3 ounces) **apricot gelatin**
2½ teaspoons **ground cinnamon**
1 teaspoon **ground cloves**

ADDITIONAL INGREDIENT:
1 cup **boiling water**

In a bowl, combine the first seven ingredients; mix well. Store in an airtight container in a cool, dry place for up to 6 months. **Yield:** 50 batches (about 5 cups total). **To prepare 1 cup of tea:** Dissolve 4½ teaspoons tea mix in boiling water; stir well.

Cool Waters Shake

Ride a wave of approval when you serve this refreshing berry-flavored beverage from the Taste of Home Test Kitchen. Kids will love its pastel blue color and seafoamy consistency... and with just three simple ingredients, it's a breeze to whip up in the blender.

4 cups **cold milk**
2 packages (3 ounces *each*) **berry blue gelatin**
1 quart **vanilla ice cream**

In a blender, combine 2 cups of milk, one package of gelatin and 2 cups of ice cream. Cover and process for 30 seconds or until smooth. Repeat. Pour into glasses and serve immediately. **Yield:** 6 servings.

Hot Cocoa Mix

"I first tasted this warming beverage on a camping trip in the mountains," recalls Ruby Gibson of Newton, North Carolina. *"It was a wonderful treat on those crisp mornings."*

6⅔ cups nonfat dry milk powder
1 cup instant chocolate drink mix
1 package (5 ounces) cook-and-serve chocolate pudding mix
½ cup confectioners' sugar
½ cup powdered nondairy creamer
½ cup baking cocoa

ADDITIONAL INGREDIENTS:
1 cup boiling water
Miniature marshmallows, optional

In a bowl, combine the first six ingredients. Store in an airtight container in a cool, dry place for up to 3 months. **Yield:** 21 batches (about 7 cups total). **To prepare hot cocoa:** Dissolve ⅓ cup cocoa mix in boiling water. Top with miniature marshmallows if desired. **Yield:** 1 serving per batch.

Frosty Orange Drink

"If you're looking for a refreshing drink, I can guarantee that you'll find it in an orange frosty," writes Karen Radford, age 12, of Bothell, Washington. *"This drink tastes delicious and is easy to make in the blender."*

1 cup water
1 cup milk
½ cup orange breakfast drink mix
½ cup sugar
1 teaspoon vanilla extract
10–12 ice cubes

Combine all ingredients in a blender; cover and process until smooth. Serve immediately. **Yield:** 4 servings.

Kool-Aid Floats

"Youngsters love this refreshing punch," says Carthage, New York's Margaret Bossuot. Sweet sherbet, fruity soft drink mix and orange juice concentrate make this beverage a popular way to beat the heat on summer days.

3 **envelopes unsweetened strawberry Kool-Aid**
3 **cups sugar**
6 **quarts cold water**
1 **can (12 ounces) frozen orange juice concentrate, thawed**
1 **liter ginger ale, chilled**
1 **quart raspberry *or* orange sherbet**

In large pitcher, prepare Kool-Aid with sugar and water according to package directions. Stir in the orange juice concentrate. Just before serving, add the ginger ale. Pour into tall glasses. Add scoops of sherbet to glasses. **Yield:** 2 gallons.

CHAPTER 2

Breakfast & Brunch

Bacon and Cheese Waffles

Pancake mix gives a jump start to this hearty hurry-up breakfast from MarGenne Rowley of Oasis, Utah. "Including bacon and cheese in the waffle batter makes an all-in-one breakfast flavor," she assures. Freeze extras to reheat another day.

1 egg
1 cup milk
1 cup (8 ounces) sour cream
1 tablespoon butter, melted
2 cups pancake *or* biscuit/baking mix
6–8 bacon strips, cooked and crumbled
1 cup (4 ounces) shredded cheddar cheese

In a medium bowl, beat egg; add milk, sour cream and butter. Stir in pancake mix; mix well. Fold in bacon and cheese. Bake in a preheated waffle iron according to manufacturer's directions until golden brown. **Yield:** 12 waffles (4-inch square).

Ham 'n' Cheese Wedges

Baking mix is a short-cut in this savory round loaf from Marietta Slater of Augusta, Kansas. "We enjoy it for breakfast, and I like to serve big wedges with a bowl of soup at lunchtime," she writes.

2 cups biscuit/baking mix
2 eggs
⅔ cup milk
2 tablespoons finely chopped onion
1 tablespoon vegetable oil
½ teaspoon prepared mustard
1¼ cups (5 ounces) shredded cheddar cheese, *divided*
1 cup cubed fully cooked ham
1 tablespoon butter, melted
2 tablespoons sesame seeds

In a mixing bowl, combine the first six ingredients; mix well. Stir in 1 cup cheese and the ham. Spread in a greased 10-in. quiche dish or pie plate. Brush with butter; sprinkle with sesame seeds. Bake at 350° for 30–35 minutes or until set and lightly browned. Sprinkle with remaining cheese. Bake 5–10 minutes longer or until the cheese is melted. Let stand for 5 minutes before cutting. Serve warm. **Yield:** 6–8 servings.

Tutti-Frutti Waffles

Pineapple and pecans are the "secret" ingredients that give these light waffles their fruity flavor and nice nutty crunch. Bev Uken of Raymond, Minnesota says "It takes just minutes to mix up the batter, then bake in a waffle iron. Topped with colorful fresh fruit, these pretty waffles are perfect for serving anytime of day."

2 cups biscuit/baking mix
2 eggs, lightly beaten
½ cup vegetable oil
1⅓ cups club soda
¼ cup crushed pineapple, drained
¼ cup chopped pecans
1 pint fresh raspberries, optional
2 medium ripe bananas, sliced, optional

In a mixing bowl, combine biscuit mix, eggs and oil. Add soda and stir until smooth. Gently fold in pineapple and pecans. Bake in a preheated waffle iron according to manufacturer's directions until golden brown. Top with raspberries and bananas if desired. **Yield:** 6–7 waffles (about 6¾ inches).

Maple-Bacon Oven Pancake

"For years, my mother has served this tasty baked pancake for dinner," says Kari Caven of Moscow, Idaho. *"But it's so quick and easy I like to make it for breakfast, too. Leftovers taste just as good the next day warmed up in the microwave."*

1½ cups biscuit/baking mix
1 tablespoon sugar
¾ cup milk
2 eggs
¼ cup maple syrup
1½ cups (6 ounces) shredded cheddar cheese, *divided*
½ pound sliced bacon, cooked and crumbled
Additional syrup, optional

In a mixing bowl, combine biscuit mix, sugar, milk, eggs, syrup and ½ cup cheese; mix well. Pour into a greased 13-in. × 9-in. × 2-in. baking dish. Bake, uncovered, at 425° for 10–15 minutes or until a toothpick inserted near the center comes out clean. Sprinkle with bacon and remaining cheese. Bake 3-5 minutes longer or until cheese is melted. Serve with syrup if desired. **Yield:** 12 servings.

Rippled Coffee Cake

In Portland, Tennessee, Jane Lear adds a fun layer of brown sugar and cinnamon to a yellow cake mix. "This delicious glazed treat is good for breakfast or dessert," she assures.

1 package (18¼ ounces) yellow cake mix
1 cup (8 ounces) sour cream
4 eggs
⅔ cup vegetable oil
1 cup packed brown sugar
1 tablespoon ground cinnamon

ICING:
2 cups confectioners' sugar
¼ cup milk
2 teaspoons vanilla extract

In a mixing bowl, combine cake mix, sour cream, eggs and oil; beat well. Spread half of the batter into a greased 13-in. × 9-in. × 2-in. baking pan. Combine brown sugar and cinnamon; sprinkle over batter. Carefully spread remaining batter on top. Bake at 350° for 30–35 minutes or until a toothpick inserted near the center comes out clean. Combine icing ingredients and drizzle over warm cake. **Yield:** 16–20 servings.

Pull-Apart Bacon Bread

"I stumbled across this recipe while looking for something different to take to a brunch," explains Traci Collins of Cheyenne, Wyoming. *"Boy, am I glad I did! Everyone asked for the recipe and could not believe it only called for five ingredients. It's the perfect item to bake for an informal get-together."*

12 bacon strips, diced
1 loaf (1 pound) frozen
   bread dough, thawed
2 tablespoons olive oil,
   divided
1 cup (4 ounces) shredded
   mozzarella cheese
1 envelope (1 ounce) ranch
   salad dressing mix

In a skillet, cook bacon over medium heat for 5 minutes or until partially cooked; drain on paper towels. Roll out dough to ½-in. thickness; brush with 1 tablespoon of oil. Cut into 1-in. pieces; place in a large bowl. Add the bacon, cheese, dressing mix and remaining oil; toss to coat. Arrange pieces in a 9-in. × 5-in. oval on a greased baking sheet, layering as needed. Cover and let rise in a warm place for 30 minutes or until doubled. Bake at 350° for 15 minutes. Cover with foil; bake 5–10 minutes longer or until golden brown. **Yield:** 1 loaf.

Bacon Quiche

Enjoy the traditional flavor of a bacon quiche without the effort by preparing this quick version from Helen Hoppes of Wabash, Indiana. Using baking mix means there's no need to fuss over a pastry crust.

3 eggs
1½ cups milk
¼ cup butter, melted
½ cup biscuit/baking mix
Dash pepper
8 bacon strips, cooked and crumbled
¾ cup shredded cheddar cheese

In a blender, combine eggs, milk and butter. Add biscuit mix and pepper; cover and process for 15 seconds. Pour into a greased 9-in. pie plate. Top with bacon and cheese. Bake at 350° for 30–35 minutes or until a knife inserted near the center comes out clean. Let stand for 10 minutes before cutting. **Yield:** 6-8 servings.

Sausage Cheese Puffs

"People are always surprised when I tell them there are only four ingredients in these tasty bite-size puffs, notes Della Moore of Troy, New York. "Cheesy and spicy, the golden morsels are a fun novelty at a breakfast or brunch …and they also make yummy party appetizers!"

1 pound bulk Italian sausage
3 cups biscuit/baking mix
4 cups (16 ounces) shredded cheddar cheese
¾ cup water

In a skillet, cook and crumble sausage until no longer pink; drain. In a bowl, combine biscuit mix and cheese; stir in sausage. Add water and toss with a fork until moistened. Shape into 1½-in. balls. Place 2 in. apart on ungreased baking sheets. Bake at 400° for 12–15 minutes or until puffed and golden brown. Cool on wire racks. **Yield:** about 4 dozen. **Editor's Note:** Baked puffs may be frozen; reheat at 400° for 7–9 minutes or until heated through (they do not need to be thawed first).

Mini Ham Quiches

"These cute quiches are easy to fix for an after-church brunch when you don't want to fuss," relates Marilou Robinson of Portland, Oregon. "They're versatile, too. Replace the ham with bacon, sausage, chicken or shrimp…or substitute chopped onion, red pepper or zucchini for the olives," she suggests.

¾ cup diced fully cooked ham
½ cup shredded sharp cheddar cheese
½ cup chopped ripe olives
3 eggs, beaten
1 cup half-and-half cream
¼ cup butter, melted
3 drops hot pepper sauce
½ cup biscuit/baking mix
2 tablespoons grated Parmesan cheese
½ teaspoon ground mustard

In a bowl, combine the ham, cheddar cheese and olives; divide among 12 greased muffin cups. In a mixing bowl, combine the remaining ingredients just until blended. Pour over ham mixture. Bake at 375° for 20–25 minutes or until a knife inserted near the center comes out clean. Let stand for 5 minutes before serving. **Yield:** 1 dozen.

Raspberry Coffee Cake

"Raspberries are abundant at our summer home on nearby Aziscohos Lake," shares Marian Cummings of West Paris, Maine. "So I developed this recipe to share the bounty with our guests. The pretty crumb-topped cake's fruity flavor really shines through."

1 cup plus 3 tablespoons sugar, *divided*
¼ cup cornstarch
3 cups fresh *or* frozen unsweetened raspberries
2 cups biscuit/baking mix
⅔ cup milk
2 eggs
2 tablespoons vegetable oil

TOPPING:
1 package (3.4 ounces) instant vanilla pudding mix
½ cup sugar
¼ cup cold butter

In a saucepan, combine 1 cup of sugar and cornstarch. Add raspberries; bring to a boil over medium heat. Boil for 2 minutes, stirring constantly. Remove from the heat; allow to cool. Meanwhile, in a mixing bowl, combine the biscuit mix, milk, eggs, oil and remaining sugar; mix well. Spread two-thirds of the batter into a greased 13-in. × 9-in. × 2-in. baking pan. Spread with raspberry mixture. Spoon remaining batter over top. For topping, combine pudding mix and sugar. Cut in butter until crumbly; sprinkle over batter. Bake at 350° for 35–40 minutes. **Yield:** 12 servings.

Frosted Cinnamon Rolls

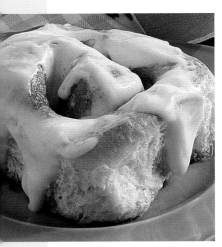

1 cup milk (70° to 80°)
¼ cup water (70° to 80°)
¼ cup butter, softened
1 egg
1 teaspoon salt
4 cups bread flour
¼ cup instant vanilla pudding mix
1 tablespoon sugar
1 tablespoon active dry yeast

FILLING:
¼ cup butter, softened
1 cup packed brown sugar
2 teaspoons ground cinnamon

FROSTING:
4 ounces cream cheese, softened
¼ cup butter, softened
1½ cups confectioners' sugar
1½ teaspoons milk
½ teaspoon vanilla extract

"These pretty cinnamon rolls are absolutely marvelous and taste just like the ones sold at the mall," notes Velma Horton of La Grange, California. *"Topped with a sweet cream cheese frosting, they're best served warm with steaming cups of coffee. Or reheat leftover rolls in the microwave and enjoy anytime of day."*

In bread machine pan, place first nine ingredients in order suggested by manufacturer. Select dough setting (check dough after 5 minutes of mixing; add 1 to 2 tablespoons water or flour if needed). When cycle is completed, turn dough onto lightly floured surface. Roll into a 17-in. × 10-in. rectangle. Spread with butter; sprinkle with brown sugar and cinnamon. Roll up jelly-roll style, starting from a long side; pinch seam to seal. Cut into 21 slices. Place 12 slices, cut side down, in a greased 13-in. × 9-in. × 2-in. baking pan and nine rolls in a 9-in. square baking pan. Cover; let rise in a warm place until doubled, about 45 minutes. Bake at 350° for 20–25 minutes or until golden brown. Cool on wire racks for 5 minutes. In a mixing bowl, beat frosting ingredients. Frost warm rolls. Store in refrigerator. **Yield:** 21 rolls. **Editor's note:** If your bread machine has a timer feature, we recommend you do not use it for this recipe.

Praline Biscuits

"These upside-down biscuits have an appealing nut topping that adds a special touch to a company brunch," says Merrill Powers of Spearville, Kansas. Best of all, they bake in just minutes.

½ cup butter, melted
½ cup packed brown sugar
36 pecan halves
Ground cinnamon
2 cups biscuit/baking mix
⅓ cup unsweetened applesauce
⅓ cup milk

Grease 12 muffin cups. In each cup, place 2 teaspoons butter, 2 teaspoons brown sugar, three pecan halves and a dash of cinnamon. In a bowl, combine biscuit mix, applesauce and milk just until moistened. Spoon into muffin cups. Bake at 450° for 10 minutes. Immediately invert onto a serving platter. Serve warm. **Yield:** 1 dozen.

Banana-Nut Corn Bread

A boxed corn bread mix gets a tasty treatment from Janice France of Depauw, Indiana when dressed up with bananas and chopped walnuts. The moist, golden loaves are a great addition to a brunch buffet or bake sale.

2 packages (8½ ounces *each*) corn bread/muffin mix
1 cup mashed ripe bananas (about 2 medium)
1 cup chopped walnuts
1 cup milk

In a bowl, combine all ingredients just until blended. Spoon into two greased 8-in. × 4-in. × 2-in. loaf pans. Bake at 350° for 35–40 minutes or until a toothpick inserted near the center comes out clean. Cool for 10 minutes before removing from pans to wire racks to cool completely. **Yield:** 2 loaves.

Sweet Raspberry Muffins

"I like to linger over a cup of coffee and a warm sweet treat on weekend mornings," says Teresa Raab of Tustin, Michigan. *"These moist muffins are perfect because making them ties up so little time in the kitchen. I also serve them with holiday meals for something different."*

2 cups biscuit/baking mix
2 tablespoons sugar
¼ cup cold butter
⅔ cup milk
¼ cup raspberry jam

GLAZE:
½ cup confectioners' sugar
2 teaspoons warm water
¼ teaspoon vanilla extract

In a bowl, combine biscuit mix and sugar. Cut in butter until the mixture resembles coarse crumbs. Stir in milk just until moistened (batter will be thick). Spoon about 1 tablespoon of batter into 12 paper-lined muffin cups. Top with 1 teaspoon jam. Spoon the remaining batter (about 1 tablespoon each) over jam. Bake at 425° for 12–14 minutes or until lightly browned. Cool in pans for 5 minutes. Meanwhile, in a small bowl, combine glaze ingredients until smooth. Remove muffins to a wire rack. Drizzle with glaze. **Yield:** 1 dozen.

Peanut Butter Pancakes

"Pancakes are one of my husband's specialties," says Dorothy Pritchett of Wills Point, Texas. *"So it's not unusual for him to wake me with these hot-from-the-griddle cakes that get their delicious difference from peanut butter."*

1 cup pancake mix
2 tablespoons sugar
1 egg
⅓ cup peanut butter
1 can (5 ounces) evaporated milk
⅓ cup water

HONEY BUTTER:
¼ cup butter, softened
2 tablespoons honey

In a bowl, combine pancake mix and sugar. In a small bowl, beat egg and peanut butter; add milk and water. Stir into dry ingredients just until moistened. Pour batter by ¼ cupfuls onto a lightly greased medium-hot griddle. Turn when bubbles form on top of pancakes; cook until second side is golden brown. Combine butter and honey in a small bowl. Serve with the pancakes. **Yield:** 10 pancakes. **Editor's Note:** This recipe was tested with Jif brand peanut butter.

Apple Custard Coffee Cake

"Once you try this luscious coffee cake, your mouth will water just thinking about it," relates Vickie Tinsley of Boonville, Missouri. *"It can be served as a dessert by simply topping squares with whipped cream and cinnamon."*

2 cups biscuit/baking mix
1 cup sugar, *divided*
¾ cup milk
1 teaspoon vanilla extract
1 cup chopped pecans
2 medium tart apples, peeled and chopped
1 teaspoon ground cinnamon, *divided*
3 eggs
1 cup heavy whipping cream

In a bowl, combine biscuit mix, ¼ cup sugar, milk and vanilla; mix well. Stir in pecans. Pour into a greased 9-in. square baking dish. Toss apples with ¼ cup sugar and ½ teaspoon of cinnamon. Sprinkle over batter. In a bowl, combine eggs, cream and remaining sugar. Pour over the apples; sprinkle with remaining cinnamon. Bake, uncovered, at 350° for 40–45 minutes or until a knife inserted near the center comes out clean. Serve warm. Refrigerate leftovers. **Yield:** 9 servings.

Mini Coffee Cakes

⅓ cup butter, softened
¼ cup sugar
1 egg
1½ cups all-purpose flour
1 package (3.4 ounces) instant vanilla pudding mix
1 tablespoon baking powder
¼ teaspoon salt
1¼ cups milk
½ cup chopped walnuts

TOPPING:
½ cup chopped walnuts
⅓ cup packed brown sugar
2 tablespoons butter, melted
¼ teaspoon ground cinnamon

"These moist, buttery muffins with their nutty topping are so easy to make," assures Dena Engelland from Sterling, Kansas. Stir up a batch of the cakes and let them bake while you prepare breakfast or brunch.

In a mixing bowl, cream butter and sugar. Beat in egg. Combine flour, pudding mix, baking powder and salt; add to the creamed mixture alternately with milk. Beat until blended. Stir in walnuts. Fill paper-lined muffin cups two-thirds full. Combine topping ingredients; sprinkle over batter. Bake at 375° for 20–25 minutes or until a toothpick inserted near the center comes out clean. Cool for 10 minutes; remove from pan to a wire rack. **Yield:** about 1 dozen.

Sausage Brunch Muffins

From Rockland, Massachusetts, Beverly Borges shares this recipe for zippy muffins chock-full of sausage. "They've become a Sunday-morning standard whenever the family gathers," she informs. "They also make a hearty hurry-up breakfast on the run."

1 pound bulk pork sausage
4 cups biscuit/baking mix
¾ cup milk
½ cup water
1 can (4 ounces) diced green chilies, undrained
1 egg, beaten
1 can (11 ounces) whole kernel corn, drained

In a skillet over medium heat, brown sausage. Drain and set aside. In a large bowl, combine biscuit mix, milk, water, chilies and egg; mix well. Stir in the corn and sausage. Fill greased or paper-lined muffin cups two-thirds full. Bake at 425° for 16–18 minutes or until golden brown. Cool for 5 minutes; remove from pan to a wire rack. Serve warm. **Yield:** 2 dozen.

Sausage Cheese Muffins

"These small savory muffins are fun to serve as appetizers or at brunch," writes Willa Paget of Nashville, Tennessee. "With just five ingredients, the tasty bites are easy to whip up to take to a party, the office or a sick friend."

1 pound bulk hot pork sausage
1 can (10¾ ounces) condensed cheddar cheese soup, undiluted
½ cup milk
2–3 teaspoons rubbed sage
3 cups biscuit/baking mix

In a skillet over medium heat, cook sausage until no longer pink; drain. In a bowl, combine soup, milk, sage and sausage. Stir in the biscuit mix just until moistened. Fill greased miniature or regular muffin cups two-thirds full. Bake at 400° for 15–20 minutes or until a toothpick comes out clean. **Yield:** 4 dozen mini-muffins or 2 dozen regular muffins.

Smiley Face Pancakes

"The batter is easy for kids of all ages to stir up," says Janette Garner of Carmel, Indiana. "Adding food coloring to small portions of the batter creates the bright facial features. Youngsters are likely to have as much fun making the tender and tasty treats as they do eating them!"

2 cups biscuit/baking mix
1¼ cups milk
1 egg, beaten
2 tablespoons sugar
2 tablespoons lemon juice
1 teaspoon vanilla extract
Red, green, yellow and blue liquid *or* paste food coloring
Maple syrup, optional

In a bowl, combine the biscuit mix, milk, egg, sugar, lemon juice and vanilla; mix until smooth. Place 1 tablespoon of batter each in four bowls. Color one red, one green, one yellow and one blue. Drop remaining batter by ¼ cupfuls onto a lightly greased hot griddle. To create faces, paint colored batter on pancakes with a new small paintbrush. Cook until bubbles form on the top. Turn and cook until second side is golden. Serve with syrup if desired. **Yield:** about 1 dozen.

Simple Sticky Buns

"I prepare these nutty rolls every Christmas Eve," reports Tyan Cadwell of St. Johns, Michigan. "Then I pop them in the oven while we're opening gifts on Christmas morning. They smell delicious while baking."

2 loaves (1 pound each) frozen bread dough, thawed, *divided*
Ground cinnamon to taste
½ cup butter
1 cup packed brown sugar
1 package (5.9 ounces) cook-and-serve vanilla pudding mix
2 tablespoons milk
1 cup chopped pecans
½ cup raisins, optional

Cut each loaf of dough into 18 pieces. Arrange half in a greased 13-in. × 9-in. × 2-in. baking dish. Sprinkle with cinnamon. In a saucepan over low heat, melt butter. Remove from the heat; stir in brown sugar, pudding mix and milk until smooth. Pour over dough. Sprinkle with pecans and raisins if desired. Arrange remaining pieces of dough over top. Cover and refrigerate overnight or let stand at room temperature for 3 hours. Bake, uncovered, at 350° for 35 minutes or until center sounds hollow when tapped with fingers. Invert onto a serving platter or baking sheet. **Yield:** 12–15 servings. **Editor's Note:** Frozen dinner roll dough (24 rolls) may be substituted for 2 loaves of bread dough.

Pecan Poppy Seed Loaves

"This bread is wonderful for brunch or with a cup of tea or coffee," notes Jean Switzer of Pauline, South Carolina. *"I keep a few loaves on hand in case friends drop in,"* she adds. *"Wrapped in foil, they stay moist for quite a while."*

2 tablespoons poppy seeds
1 cup hot water
1 package (18¼ ounces) yellow cake mix
1 package (3.4 ounces) instant coconut cream *or* lemon pudding mix
4 eggs
½ cup vegetable oil
½ cup chopped pecans, toasted

In a mixing bowl, combine poppy seeds and water. Add cake and pudding mixes, eggs and oil. Beat on medium speed for 2 minutes. Stir in pecans. Pour into two greased 8-in. × 4-in. × 2-in. loaf pans. Bake at 350° for 45–50 minutes or until a toothpick inserted near the center comes out clean. Cool for 10 minutes; remove from pans to wire racks to cool completely. **Yield:** 2 loaves.

CHAPTER 3

Salads & Side Dishes

Berry Gelatin Ring

Cranberries give extra holiday appeal to this gelatin salad sent in by Elise Spring of Bellevue, Ohio. "A co-worker always shares this festive fruit ring with us at staff potlucks," she relates.

1 package (6 ounces) raspberry gelatin
2 cups boiling water
1 can (16 ounces) whole-berry cranberry sauce
1 can (8 ounces) crushed pineapple, undrained
½ cup red wine *or* grape juice
⅓ cup chopped walnuts
1 package (8 ounces) cream cheese, softened
¼ cup mayonnaise
1 teaspoon grated orange peel

In a bowl, dissolve gelatin in water. Add cranberry sauce, pineapple, wine or juice and walnuts; mix well. To evenly distribute fruit and nuts, chill until partially set, about 2 hours. Then pour into a 6-cup ring mold coated with non-stick cooking spray. Refrigerate until set. Unmold onto a serving plate. In a small mixing bowl, combine cream cheese, mayonnaise and orange peel. Serve with the salad. **Yield:** 8 servings.

Vegetable Rice Medley

"Here's a side dish that's easy to make because it uses convenience foods," notes Coleen Martin of Brookfield, Wisconsin. "Mixed frozen vegetables eliminate any need for chopping, and the onion soup mix adds great flavor to the rice."

1 cup uncooked long grain rice
2¼ cups water
2–3 tablespoons onion *or* vegetable soup mix
¼ teaspoon salt
2 cups frozen corn, peas *or* mixed vegetables

In a saucepan, combine the rice, water, soup mix and salt; bring to a boil. Add the vegetables; return to a boil. Reduce heat; cover and simmer for 15 minutes. Cook until rice and vegetables are tender. **Yield:** 4–6 servings.

Colorful Vegetable Bake

"My sister gave me the recipe for this side dish years ago, and it's become a favorite in our household," writes *Betty Brown from Buckley, Washington. Chock-full of colorful veggies, it's delicious and feeds a crowd.*

3 cups frozen cut green beans, thawed and drained
2 medium green peppers, chopped
6 plum tomatoes, chopped and seeded
2–3 cups (8 to 12 ounces) shredded cheddar cheese
3 cups chopped zucchini
1 cup biscuit/baking mix
½ teaspoon salt
½ teaspoon cayenne pepper
6 eggs
1 cup milk

Place beans and peppers in a greased 13-in. × 9-in. × 2-in. baking dish. Top with tomatoes, cheese and zucchini. In a bowl, combine the biscuit mix, salt, cayenne, eggs and milk just until moistened. Pour over the vegetables. Bake, uncovered, at 350° for 55–60 minutes or until puffed and a knife inserted near the center comes out clean. Let stand for 10 minutes before serving. **Yield:** 12 servings.

Corn Bread Casserole

"While this side dish is baking, I can fix the rest of our dinner," notes Carrina Cooper of McAlpin, Florida. *"It's easy to add variety by stirring in cooked crumbled bacon. Since my husband likes spicy foods, I frequently sprinkle chopped jalapeno peppers over half of the dish for him."*

1 can (15¼ ounces) whole kernel corn, drained
1 can (14¾ ounces) cream-style corn
1 package (8½ ounces) corn bread/muffin mix
1 egg
2 tablespoons butter, melted
¼ teaspoon garlic powder
¼ teaspoon paprika

In a large bowl, combine all ingredients. Pour into a greased 11-in. × 7-in. × 2-in. baking dish. Bake, uncovered, at 400° for 25–30 minutes or until the top and edges are golden brown. **Yield:** 4–6 servings.

Jalapeno Appetizer Pancakes

Jalapeno peppers and mozzarella cheese give a tasty twist to these bite-size pancakes made from a mix. "My grandchildren love them with ranch dress-ing for dipping," says Lorraine Watson of Malta, Montana.

2 cups pancake mix
1½ cups water
2 cups (8 ounces) shredded mozzarella cheese
1 can (4 ounces) diced jalapeno peppers, drained
Ranch salad dressing *or* salsa

In a bowl, combine pancake mix and water; mix well. Stir in cheese and peppers. Pour the batter by heaping tablespoon-fuls onto a greased hot griddle; turn when bubbles form on top of pancakes. Cook until second side is golden brown. Serve warm with dressing or salsa. **Yield:** about 2½ dozen.

Creamy Italian Noodles

From Moundville, Missouri, Linda Hendrix sends an easy recipe for no-fail noodles that are a flavorful accompaniment to most any meat. Rich and creamy, they're special enough for company, too.

1 package (8 ounces) wide egg noodles
¼ cup butter, softened
½ cup heavy whipping cream, half-and-half cream *or* evaporated milk
¼ cup grated Parmesan cheese
2¼ teaspoons Italian salad dressing mix

Cook noodles according to package directions; drain and place in a bowl. Toss with butter. Add the remaining ingredients and mix well. Serve immediately. **Yield:** 4–6 servings.

Stuffing Baskets

This super-easy side dish from the Taste of Home Test Kitchen dresses up instant stuffing mix with pecans, green peppers and mushrooms for hearty flavor. The "baskets" are solid color or holiday-themed paper muffin liners.

1 medium green pepper, chopped
¼ cup butter
1 jar (4½ ounces) sliced mushrooms
1 package (6 ounces) instant stuffing mix
½ cup chopped pecans

In a saucepan, saute green pepper in butter until crisp-tender. Drain mushrooms, reserving liquid; set mushrooms aside. Add water to liquid to measure 1⅔ cups. Add to green pepper. Bring to a boil; stir in the stuffing mix. Remove from the heat. Cover and let stand for 5 minutes. Add mushrooms and pecans; fluff with a fork. Spoon into paper-lined muffin cups; pack lightly. Bake at 350° for 30–35 minutes. **Yield:** 1 dozen.

Pizza Potatoes

"For a simple side dish that's sure to appeal to kids, try this twist on traditional pizza," advises Kathy White of Chicopee, Massachusetts. Packaged scalloped potatoes, canned tomatoes and pepperoni slices are combined for fast Italian fare.*

1 package (5 ounces) scalloped potatoes
1 can (14½ ounces) Italian stewed tomatoes
1½ cups water
¼ teaspoon dried oregano
1 package (3½ ounces) sliced pepperoni
1 cup (4 ounces) shredded mozzarella cheese

Combine the potatoes and contents of sauce mix in a greased 1½-qt. baking dish. In a saucepan, bring tomatoes, water and oregano to a boil. Pour over potatoes. Top with pepperoni. Bake, uncovered, at 375° for 50–60 minutes or until the potatoes are tender. Sprinkle with cheese. Bake 5–10 minutes longer or until cheese is melted. **Yield:** 4 servings.

Frosted Gelatin Salad

A sweet, creamy topping frosts this extra-fruity gelatin that is chock-full of canned apricots and crushed pineapple. "It's a colorful salad to serve at potluck dinners," reports Bertha Johnson of Indianapolis, Indiana. "Everyone loves the combination of flavors."

1 package (6 ounces) orange gelatin
2 cups boiling water
¾ cup miniature marshmallows
2 cans (17 ounces *each*) apricot halves, undrained
1 can (20 ounces) crushed pineapple, drained
½ cup sugar
3 tablespoons all-purpose flour
1 egg, beaten
1 teaspoon vanilla extract
2 envelopes whipped topping mix
¼ cup finely shredded cheddar cheese

In a bowl, dissolve gelatin in boiling water. Add marshmallows; stir until melted. Drain apricots, reserving 1 cup juice; set juice aside. Chop apricots; add to gelatin with pineapple. Pour into an 11-in. × 7-in. × 2-in. dish. Chill until firm. Meanwhile, in a saucepan, combine the sugar and flour. Whisk in egg, vanilla and reserved apricot juice until smooth. Bring to a boil; boil and stir for 2 minutes. Cool completely. Prepare whipped topping according to package directions; fold in cooled juice mixture. Spread over gelatin. Sprinkle with cheese. Chill for 1 hour. **Yield:** 12 servings

Cran-Raspberry Gelatin

You'll love the sweet-tart flavor and beautiful ruby-red color of this chunky fruit salad from Kathy Jarvis of Bear Creek, Wisconsin. "It's great served with a Thanksgiving turkey," she notes.

1 package (3 ounces) raspberry gelatin
1½ cups boiling water
1 cup fresh *or* frozen cranberries
½ cup raspberry jam *or* spreadable fruit
1 can (8 ounces) crushed pineapple, undrained

In a bowl, dissolve gelatin in water. Place cranberries, jam and gelatin mixture in a blender or food processor; cover and process until cranberries are coarsely chopped. Transfer to a bowl; stir in pineapple. Refrigerate until set. **Yield:** 8 servings.

Herbed Tossed Salad

Deb Morrison of Skiatook, Oklahoma uses a salad dressing mix to get a jump start on preparing this colorful salad. "I add fresh basil from my garden," she explains, "which gives it a flavor boost."

8 cups torn lettuce
1 cup fresh cilantro, coarsely chopped
1 cup sliced fresh mushrooms
2 medium tomatoes, chopped
1 medium carrot, shredded
2 radishes, sliced
1 envelope Italian salad dressing mix
1 tablespoon minced fresh basil *or* 1 teaspoon
   dried basil
1 garlic clove, minced

In a large bowl, toss the lettuce, cilantro, mushrooms, tomatoes, carrot and radishes. Prepare salad dressing according to package directions; add basil and garlic. Pour over the salad and toss to coat. **Yield:** 6–8 servings.

Hush Puppy Mix

*Edna Bullett of
Wilburton, Oklahoma
adds garlic powder
and red pepper flakes
to the cornmeal mix
that creates these
golden hush puppies.
"You'll win rave reviews
for the crunchy crust
and spicy flavor of these
corn-filled bites," she
promises.*

4⅓ cups self-rising cornmeal mix
2 tablespoons sugar
2 tablespoons garlic powder
1 tablespoon pepper
1 teaspoon salt
½ teaspoon crushed red pepper flakes

ADDITIONAL INGREDIENTS:
1 can (8½ ounces) cream-style corn
½ cup chopped onion
1 egg
Oil for deep-fat frying

In a bowl, combine the first six ingredients; mix well. Store in an airtight container in a cool, dry place for up to 6 months. **Yield:** 3 batches (4½ cups total). **To prepare hush puppies:** In a bowl, combine 1½ cups mix, corn, onion and egg; stir just until moistened. In an electric skillet or deep-fat fryer, heat 1½ in. of oil to 375°. Drop batter by teaspoonfuls into oil; fry until golden brown. Drain on paper towels. Serve warm. **Yield:** about 4 dozen per batch. **Editor's Note:** There is no substitute for self-rising cornmeal mix.

Squash Stuffing Casserole

"The recipe for this zippy side dish was given to me by my husband's grandmother." reports Tara Kay Cottingham of Munday, Texas. *Convenient corn bread stuffing mix and a can of green chilies give fast flavor to sliced summer squash.* "Since I cook for just my husband and me, I often freeze the leftovers for another day," *she says.*

¾ cup water
¼ teaspoon salt
6 cups sliced yellow summer squash (¼ inch thick)
1 small onion, halved and sliced
1 can (10¾ ounces) condensed cream of mushroom soup, undiluted
1 cup (8 ounces) sour cream
1 package (6 ounces) instant corn bread stuffing mix
1 can (4 ounces) chopped green chilies
Salt and pepper to taste
1 cup (4 ounces) shredded cheddar cheese

In a large saucepan, bring water and salt to a boil. Add squash and onion. Reduce heat; cover and cook until squash is crisp-tender, about 6 minutes. Drain well; set aside. In a bowl, combine soup, sour cream, stuffing and the contents of seasoning packet, chilies, salt and pepper; mix well. Fold in squash mixture. Pour into a greased shallow 2-qt. baking dish. Sprinkle with cheese. Bake, uncovered, at 350° for 25–30 minutes or until heated through. **Yield:** 8–10 servings.

Fruit Cocktail Salad

"Convenient canned fruit and instant pudding mix streamline preparation of this refreshing medley," reports Karen Buhr of Gasport, New York. *This shortcut salad can also be served as a sweet, satisfying dessert for diabetics.*

2 cans (16 ounces *each*) fruit cocktail in juice, undrained
1 can (20 ounces) unsweetened pineapple tidbits, drained
1 can (11 ounces) mandarin oranges, drained
1 tablespoon lemon juice
1 package (1 ounce) instant sugar-free vanilla pudding mix
2 medium firm bananas, sliced

In a bowl, combine the fruit and lemon juice. Sprinkle with pudding mix. Stir gently for 1 minute or until mixture is thickened. Fold in bananas. Refrigerate until serving. **Yield:** 12 servings.

Special Wild Rice Salad

"A friend fixed this for a company outing a few years ago, and it has since become my favorite picnic salad," says Suzanne Strocsher of Bothell, Washington. Jars of marinated mushrooms and artichoke hearts, along with fresh vegetables, turn prepared rice mix into something special.

  2 packages (6 ounces *each*) long grain and wild rice mix
2–3 ripe avocados, peeled and chopped
  1 jar (8 ounces) marinated whole mushrooms, undrained
  1 jar (6½ ounces) marinated artichoke hearts, undrained
1–2 medium tomatoes, diced
  2 celery ribs, chopped
2–3 green onions, chopped
  ½ cup Italian salad dressing

Prepare rice according to package directions. Cool; place in a large bowl. Add remaining ingredients and toss to coat. Cover and refrigerate overnight. **Yield:** 10-12 servings.

Cottage Cheese Fluff

"Packaged gelatin and canned fruit make this salad easy to make and good to eat," assures Annette Self of Junction City, Ohio. "I vary the flavor of gelatin and type of fruit based on the rest of the meal."

  1 cup (8 ounces) small-curd cottage cheese
  1 package (3 ounces) gelatin flavor of your choice
  1 can (11 ounces) mandarin oranges, drained
  1 cup unsweetened crushed pineapple, drained
  ½ cup chopped pecans, optional
  1 carton (8 ounces) frozen whipped topping, thawed

In a bowl, combine the cottage cheese and gelatin powder; mix well. Stir in oranges, pineapple and pecans if desired. Just before serving, fold in the whipped topping. **Yield:** 8 servings.

Nutty Broccoli Slaw

"My daughter gave me the recipe for this delightful salad," says Dora Clapsaddle of Kensington, Ohio. *The sweet dressing nicely coats a crisp blend of broccoli slaw mix, carrots, onions, almonds and sunflower kernels. Crushed ramen noodles provide even more crunch. "It's a smash hit wherever I take it,"* Dora adds.

1 package (3 ounces) chicken ramen noodles
1 package (16 ounces) broccoli slaw mix
2 cups sliced green onions (about 2 bunches)
1½ cups broccoli florets
1 can (6 ounces) ripe olives, drained and halved
1 cup sunflower kernels, toasted
½ cup slivered almonds, toasted
½ cup sugar
½ cup cider vinegar
½ cup olive oil

Set aside the ramen noodle seasoning packet; crush the noodles and place in a large bowl. Add the slaw mix, onions, broccoli, olives, sunflower kernels and almonds. In a jar with a tight-fitting lid, combine the sugar, vinegar, oil and contents of seasoning packet; shake well. Drizzle over salad and toss to coat. Serve immediately. **Yield:** 16 servings.

Artichoke Rice Salad

"A close friend shared this make-ahead recipe that starts with a pack-aged rice mix," notes Sonja Blow of Grove-land, California. Curry and artichoke hearts give it a flavorful change of pace that's welcome at a picnic or potluck.

1 package (6.9 ounces) chicken-flavored rice mix
2 jars (6½ ounces *each*) marinated artichoke hearts
3 cups cooked long grain rice
3 cups chopped green onions
¾ cup mayonnaise
½ teaspoon curry powder

Prepare rice mix according to package directions; cool. Drain artichokes, reserving marinade. Chop artichokes; place in a large bowl. Add prepared rice, long grain rice and onions. In a small bowl, combine mayonnaise, curry powder and reserved marinade. Pour over rice mixture and toss to coat. Cover and refrigerate until serving. **Yield:** 10–12 servings.

Vegetable Rice Mix

In Freeport, Florida, Marjorie Carey puts together this easy rice dish flavored with veg-etable soup mix. Each batch makes a pretty side dish when you're in a hurry.

4 cups uncooked instant rice
1 package (1.4 ounces) vegetable soup mix
2 tablespoons dried minced onion
2 tablespoons dried celery flakes
2 tablespoons dried sweet red *or* green pepper
1½ teaspoons salt

ADDITIONAL INGREDIENTS:
2 cups water
1 tablespoon butter

In a bowl, combine the first six ingredients; mix well. Store in an airtight container in a cool dry place for up to 1 year. **Yield:** 4 batches (4 cups total). **To prepare rice:** In a saucepan, combine water, butter and 1 cup rice mix. Bring to a boil; reduce heat. Cover and simmer for 10–15 minutes or until the water is absorbed. **Yield:** 2–3 servings per batch.

Sailboat Salads

You can steer clear of a long list of ingredients when your family fixes these sensational salads shared by Lee Nelson of Waco, Texas. "My grandson, Sean McGowan, likes to help his mom work in the kitchen," Lee relates. "He always offers to make these delightful salads."

1 package (3 ounces) berry blue gelatin
1 cup boiling water
1 cup cold water
1 can (29 ounces) peach halves, drained
4 toothpicks
2 thick slices process American cheese
2 cups torn lettuce

Place gelatin in a bowl; add boiling water and stir until gelatin is dissolved. Stir in cold water. Pour gelatin onto four salad plates; refrigerate until firm. For boat, place a peach half, cut side up, in the center of each plate (refrigerate any remaining peaches for another use). Cut cheese slices in half diagonally. For sail, carefully insert a toothpick into the top center of each cheese triangle. Bend cheese slightly; push toothpick through bottom center of cheese. Insert toothpick into edge of peach. Arrange lettuce around plate. **Yield:** 4 servings.

Crunchy Coleslaw

"This crunchy cabbage salad is so easy to put together that we often have it for spur-of-the-moment picnics or when unexpected company stops by," remarks Julie Vavroch of Montezuma, Iowa. It gets its nutty flavor from almonds.

⅓ cup vegetable oil
1 package (3 ounces) beef-flavored ramen noodles
½ teaspoon garlic salt
1 package (16 ounces) shredded coleslaw mix
1 package (5 ounces) sliced almonds

In a small saucepan, heat oil. Stir in contents of noodle seasoning packet and garlic salt; cook for 3–4 minutes or until blended. Meanwhile, crush the noodles and place in a large bowl. Add coleslaw mix and almonds. Drizzle with oil mixture and toss to coat. Serve immediately. **Yield:** 6–8 servings.

Cider Cranberry Salad

"The area we live in grows lots of cranberries, and we really like them," comments Barbara Taylor of Ocean Park, Washington. Her gelatin salad has orange and apple flavors that accent the cranberry sauce.

1 package (3 ounces) orange gelatin
¾ cup boiling apple cider
¾ cup cold apple cider
1 can (16 ounces) whole-berry cranberry sauce

In a bowl, dissolve gelatin in boiling cider. Stir in cold cider and cranberry sauce. Pour into individual dishes. Chill until firm. **Yield:** 6–8 servings.

Glazed Carrots

Ranch salad dressing mix flavors these tasty carrots from Marion Reed of Omak, Washington. The side dish relies on packages of baby carrots, so there's no time-consuming peeling or slicing.

2 packages (16 ounces *each*) fresh baby carrots
½ cup butter
½ cup packed brown sugar
2 envelopes ranch salad dressing mix

Place carrots in a saucepan; add 1 in. of water. Bring to a boil. Reduce heat; cover and cook for 8–10 minutes or until crisp-tender. Drain and set aside. In the same pan, combine butter, brown sugar and salad dressing mix until blended. Add carrots. Cook and stir over medium heat for 5 minutes or until glazed. **Yield:** 10–12 servings.

Dilly Zucchini Casserole

"Whenever I take this time-saving side dish casserole to a potluck, I seldom bring any home, and folks often ask for the recipe," reports Esther Kilborn of Bridgton, Maine. *"If I have fresh dill, I'll substitute a couple tablespoons for the dill weed,"* she notes.

1 cup biscuit/baking mix
½ cup grated Parmesan cheese
1 tablespoon dill weed
1 teaspoon salt
⅛ teaspoon pepper
4 eggs, beaten
½ cup vegetable oil
3 cups chopped zucchini
1 large onion, chopped

In a bowl, combine biscuit mix, Parmesan cheese, dill, salt and pepper. Add eggs and oil; mix well. Stir in zucchini and onion until blended. Pour into a greased 1½-qt. baking dish. Bake, uncovered, at 375° for 25–30 minutes or until golden brown. **Yield:** 5 servings.

Jazzy Gelatin

Finish things off with a bang with this colorful gelatin garnished with a chorus of fresh grapes. Developed by the Taste of Home Test Kitchen, it's chock-full of mandarin oranges and crushed pineapple, and so refreshing that guests won't be able to refrain from having seconds.

1 package (6 ounces) orange gelatin
2 cups boiling water
1 cup ice cubes
1 can (15 ounces) mandarin oranges, drained
1 can (8 ounces) unsweetened crushed pineapple, undrained
1 can (6 ounces) frozen orange juice concentrate, thawed
Green grapes and fresh mint, optional

In a bowl, dissolve gelatin in boiling water. Add ice cubes, oranges, pineapple and orange juice concentrate. Pour into a 6-cup ring mold coated with nonstick cooking spray. Refrigerate overnight or until firm. Just before serving, unmold onto a serving plate. If desired, fill center with grapes and garnish with mint. **Yield:** 12 servings.

Gelatin Christmas Ornaments

Muffin tins are the key to making these individual gelatin salads created by the Taste of Home Test Kitchen. Once chilled, they're easy to embellish with mayonnaise, sour cream or whipped cream. Maraschino cherries with stems give the look of wire hangers.

3¼ cups white grape juice
1 package (6 ounces) lime gelatin
1 package (6 ounces) raspberry gelatin
6 *each* red and green maraschino cherries with stems
Mayonnaise, sour cream *or* whipped cream in a can

In a saucepan, bring grape juice to a boil. Place lime gelatin in a bowl; add half of the juice and stir until completely dissolved. Repeat with raspberry gelatin. Pour lime gelatin into six muffin cups (about ⅓ cup in each) coated with nonstick cooking spray. Repeat, filling six more cups with raspberry gelatin.

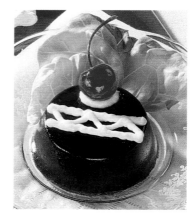

Refrigerate for 4 hours or until firm. Loosen gelatin around the edges with a sharp knife; invert muffin tin onto waxed paper. Use a metal spatula to transfer to serving plates. Fill a small plastic bag with mayonnaise; cut a small hole in corner of bag. Pipe a small circle near one edge of each ornament; place cherry in center. Decorate ornaments with additional mayonnaise if desired. **Yield:** 1 dozen.

Applesauce Gelatin Squares

"I make this attractive soft-set salad during the holidays and garnish it with ranch dressing that's tinted green," relates Judy Ernst of Montague, Michigan. "Or spoon on a dollop of whipped topping for a light, sweet dessert anytime."

4 packages (3 ounce *each*) sugar-free raspberry gelatin or flavor of your choice
4 cups boiling water
2 cups cold water
1 jar (46 ounces) unsweetened applesauce

In a bowl, dissolve gelatin in boiling water. Stir in cold water and applesauce. Pour into a 13-in. × 9-in. × 2-in. dish coated with nonstick cooking spray. Refrigerate for 8 hours or overnight. Cut into squares. **Yield:** 16 servings.

Fruit-Filled Raspberry Ring

"People love this fruity gelatin ring that gets extra flavor from an ambrosia-like mixture in the center," reports Janice Steinmetz of Somers, Connecticut. *"I've been bringing it to potlucks, buffets and showers for 20 years. While it looks like you fussed, it's easy to make the night before a special occasion."*

2 packages (6 ounces *each*) raspberry gelatin
4 cups boiling water
1 quart raspberry sherbet
1 can (14 ounces) pineapple tidbits, drained
1 can (11 ounces) mandarin oranges, drained
1 cup flaked coconut
1 cup miniature marshmallows
1 cup (8 ounces) sour cream

In a bowl, dissolve gelatin in boiling water. Stir in sherbet until melted. Pour into an 8-cup ring mold coated with nonstick cooking spray. Chill overnight or until firm. In a bowl, combine the pineapple, oranges, coconut, marshmallows and sour cream. Cover and chill. To serve, unmold gelatin onto a serving plate. Spoon fruit mixture into center of ring. **Yield:** 12–16 servings.

Cherry Gelatin Squares

"I like to take advantage of gelatin mixes and pie fillings to make colorful salads that can be prepared the day before you need them," notes Chris Rentmeister of Ripon, Wisconsin. *"These fruity squares are great for everyday suppers, yet special enough for company."*

1 package (6 ounces) cherry gelatin
1½ cups boiling water
1 can (21 ounces) cherry pie filling
1¼ cups lemon-lime soda, chilled
Whipped topping, optional

In a bowl, dissolve gelatin in water. Stir in pie filling; mix well. Slowly stir in soda (mixture will foam). Pour into an 8-in. square dish. Cover and refrigerate until firm. Cut into squares. Garnish with whipped topping if desired. **Yield:** 9 servings.

Vegetable Wild Rice

A convenient packaged rice mix gives a jump start to this simple side dish from Helen Jacobs of Canton, Michigan. A bright blend of veggies adds color.

1 package (6 ounces) long grain and wild rice mix
2 medium carrots, cut into ¼-inch slices
1 cup diced yellow summer squash
⅔ cup chopped sweet red pepper
⅔ cup chopped green pepper
¼ cup chopped onion
2 tablespoons vegetable oil

In a saucepan, place rice mix, contents of seasoning packet and water as directed on package. Bring to a boil. Add carrots. Reduce heat; cover and simmer for 30 minutes or until rice is tender and water is absorbed. Meanwhile, in a skillet, saute squash, peppers and onion in oil until crisp-tender. Stir into rice mixture. **Yield:** 6 servings.

Strawberry Rhubarb Gelatin

Rhubarb lends a hint of natural tartness to this sweet salad shared by Opal Schmidt of Battle Creek, Iowa. As a fruity side dish, its vibrant color is sure to add eye-opening appeal to almost any meal.

2 cups diced fresh *or* frozen rhubarb
½–¾ cup sugar
¼ cup water
1 package (3 ounces) strawberry gelatin
1½ cups whipped topping

In a saucepan, bring rhubarb, sugar and water to a boil. Reduce heat; simmer, uncovered, for 3–5 minutes or until the rhubarb is softened. Remove from the heat; stir in gelatin until dissolved. Pour into a bowl. Refrigerate for 20 minutes or until partially set. Fold in whipped topping. Chill until firm. **Yield:** 4 servings.

Slow Cooker Mashed Potatoes

Sour cream and cream cheese give richness to these smooth make-ahead potatoes from Trudy Vincent of Valles Mines, Missouri. "They are wonderful for Thanksgiving or Christmas dinner since there's no last-minute mashing required," she remarks.

1 package (3 ounces) cream cheese, softened
½ cup sour cream
¼ cup butter, softened
1 envelope ranch salad dressing mix
1 teaspoon dried parsley flakes
6 cups warm mashed potatoes (prepared without milk *or* butter)

In a bowl, combine the cream cheese, sour cream, butter, salad dressing mix and parsley; stir in potatoes. Transfer to a slow cooker. Cover and cook on low for 2–4 hours. **Yield:** 8–10 servings. **Editor's Note:** This recipe was tested with fresh potatoes (not instant) in a slow cooker with heating elements surrounding the unit, not only in the base.

Vegetable Rice Salad

Cathy Sestak of Freeburg, Missouri shares this mixture of leftover rice and crisp vegetables in a cool, creamy dressing. "I always receive lots of compliments when I bring this salad to parties and get-togethers," Cathy reports.

1½ cups cooked rice
1 cup broccoli florets
1 cup cauliflowerets
3 green onions, thinly sliced
½ cup mayonnaise
2 tablespoons ranch salad dressing mix
2 tablespoons milk
1 tablespoon vinegar
2 teaspoons sugar

In a bowl, combine rice, broccoli, cauliflower and onions. In a small bowl, combine the remaining ingredients; mix well. Stir into rice mixture. Cover and refrigerate for 1 hour or until serving. **Yield:** 6 servings.

Zucchini Pancakes

"In place of potato pancakes, try these cute rounds that are very simple to prepare with on-hand ingredients," says Teressa Eastman of El Dorado, Kansas. "Not only are they tasty, they're pretty, too. To eliminate some of the fat, I use a nonstick griddle coated with butter-flavored cooking spray," she advises.

⅓ cup biscuit/baking mix
¼ cup grated Parmesan cheese
⅛ teaspoon pepper
2 eggs, lightly beaten
2 cups shredded zucchini
2 tablespoons butter

In a bowl, combine the biscuit mix, Parmesan cheese, pepper and eggs just until blended. Add the zucchini; mix well. In a large skillet, melt butter. Drop batter by about ⅓ cupfuls into skillet; press lightly to flatten. Fry until golden brown, about 3 minutes on each side. **Yield:** 5 pancakes.

CHAPTER 4

Main Dishes

Steak Burritos

In Portland, Maine, Valerie Jones spices up flank steak with convenient taco seasoning packets. Slowly simmered all day, the beef is tender and a snap to shred. Just fill flour tortillas and add toppings for a tasty, time-easing meal.

2 flank steaks (about 1 pound *each*)
2 envelopes taco seasoning
1 medium onion, chopped
1 can (4 ounces) chopped green chilies
1 tablespoon vinegar
10 flour tortillas (7 inches)
1½ cups (6 ounces) shredded Monterey Jack cheese
1½ cups chopped seeded plum tomatoes
¾ cup sour cream

Cut steaks in half; rub with taco seasoning. Place in a slow cooker coated with nonstick cooking spray. Top with onion, chilies and vinegar. Cover and cook on low for 8–9 hours or until meat is tender. Remove steaks and cool slightly; shred meat with two forks. Return to slow cooker; heat through. Spoon about ½ cup meat mixture down the center of each tortilla. Top with cheese, tomato and sour cream. Fold ends and sides over filling. **Yield:** 10 servings.

Sweet 'n' Spicy Chicken

"My husband and three children love this tender chicken that has a spicy sauce," notes Sheri White of Higley, Arizona. *Peach preserves add just a touch of sweetness, while taco seasoning and salsa give this dish some kick. This entree can be made even zippier by adding more taco seasoning and using spicier salsa.*

1 pound boneless skinless chicken breasts, cut into ½-inch cubes
3 tablespoons taco seasoning
1–2 tablespoons vegetable oil
1 jar (11 ounces) chunky salsa
½ cup peach preserves
Hot cooked rice

Place the chicken in a large resealable plastic bag; add taco seasoning and toss to coat. In a skillet, brown chicken in oil. Combine salsa and preserves; stir into skillet. Bring to a boil. Reduce heat; cover and simmer for 2–3 minutes or until meat juices run clear. Serve over rice. **Yield:** 4 servings.

Quicker Chicken and Dumplings

This "quicker" version of traditional chicken and dumplings developed by the Taste of Home Test Kitchen takes less time because it uses a purchased biscuit mix and canned broth rather than homemade.

4 cups chicken broth
½ cup sliced celery
½ cup sliced carrots
1 bay leaf
1 teaspoon dried parsley flakes

DUMPLINGS:
2 cups biscuit/baking mix
¼ teaspoon dried thyme
Dash ground nutmeg
⅔ cup milk
½ teaspoon dried parsley flakes
3 cups cubed cooked chicken breast

In a 5-qt. Dutch oven or kettle, combine broth, celery, carrots, bay leaf and parsley; bring to a boil. For dumplings, combine biscuit mix, thyme and nutmeg; stir in milk and parsley just until moistened. Drop by tablespoonfuls onto the boiling broth. Cook, uncovered, for 10 minutes; cover and cook 10 minutes longer. With a slotted spoon, remove dumplings to a serving dish; keep warm. Bring broth to a boil. Reduce heat; add chicken and heat through. Remove bay leaf. Spoon chicken and broth over dumplings.
Yield: 4 servings.

Spanish Sausage Supper

"A pastor's wife shared her recipe for this colorful all-in-one skillet meal that she frequently brings to church dinners," says Gene Pitts of Wilsonville, Alabama. *"Hearty chunks of smoked sausage and canned tomatoes with chilies add just the right amount of zip to a packaged rice mix."*

½ cup chopped green pepper
⅓ cup chopped celery
¼ cup chopped onion
1 tablespoon vegetable oil
1 pound fully cooked smoked sausage, sliced
2 cups water
1 can (10 ounces) diced tomatoes and green chilies, undrained
1 package (6.8 ounces) Spanish rice and vermicelli mix
¼ cup sliced stuffed olives
⅛ teaspoon pepper

In a large skillet, saute green pepper, celery and onion in oil until tender. Add remaining ingredients; mix well. Cover and simmer for 15–20 minutes or until rice is tender and liquid is absorbed, stirring occasionally. **Yield:** 4 servings.

Tuna Alfredo

Vicki Didier of Machesney Park, Illinois, uses a packaged noodles and sauce mix to make this old-fashioned-tasting tuna casserole. "When it's just my husband and me for dinner, I rely on this fast favorite," she says.

1 package (4.4 ounces) quick-cooking Alfredo noodles and sauce mix
1 can (6 ounces) tuna, drained and flaked
1 tablespoon chopped green onion

Prepare noodles and sauce mix according to package directions. Stir in tuna and onion. Serve immediately. **Yield:** 2–3 servings. **Editor's Note:** This recipe was tested with Lipton Alfredo Mix.

Microwave Swiss Steak

Grace Ling of Winona, Minnesota lets her microwave do the work with this hassle-free Swiss steak dinner. "Because this dish is so simple to assemble, it's perfect after a long day when I don't feel like cooking," she notes.

1½ **pounds boneless round steak (¼ inch thick)**
3 **tablespoons onion soup mix**
1 **can (4 ounces) mushroom stems and pieces, drained**
1 **can (14½ ounces) diced tomatoes**
2 **tablespoons cornstarch**
¼–½ **teaspoon pepper**
Dash cayenne pepper, optional

Cut steak into serving-size pieces; pound with a mallet to tenderize. Place the steak in an ungreased shallow microwave-safe dish. Sprinkle with soup mix and mushrooms. Drain tomatoes, reserving liquid; set tomatoes aside. In a bowl, combine the cornstarch and tomato liquid until smooth. Add pepper, cayenne if desired and tomatoes. Pour over meat. Cover and microwave on high for 6–7 minutes or until mixture begins to boil. Microwave, covered, at 50% power for 20 minutes. Turn meat and rotate dish. Cover and cook at 50% power 20–25 minutes longer or until meat is tender. **Yield:** 6 servings.

Curly Noodle Pork Supper

This hearty meal-in-one from Carmen Carlson of Kent, Washington is loaded with tender pork and ramen noodles. Broccoli and red pepper add a bounty of fresh-from-the-garden flavor that will bring 'em back for seconds.

1 **pound pork tenderloin, cut into ¼-inch strips**
1 **medium sweet red pepper, cut into 1-inch pieces**
1 **cup broccoli florets**
4 **green onions, cut into 1-inch pieces**
1 **tablespoon vegetable oil**
1½ **cups water**
2 **packages (3 ounces *each*) pork ramen noodles**
1 **tablespoon minced fresh parsley**
1 **tablespoon soy sauce**

In a large skillet, cook pork, red pepper, broccoli and onions in oil until meat is no longer pink. Add the water, noodles with contents of seasoning packets, parsley and soy sauce. Bring to a boil. Reduce heat; cook for 3–4 minutes or until noodles are tender. **Yield:** 3–4 servings.

Green Bean Chicken Casserole

"My husband, who claims to be strictly a meat-and-potatoes man, asked for seconds the first time I threw together this comforting all-in-one meal," reports DeLissa Mingee of Warr Acres, Oklahoma. *"My daughter and several guests raved about it, too. It's easy to assemble with cooked chicken, frozen green beans and convenient pantry items."*

1 package (6 ounces) **long grain and wild rice mix**
4 cups **cubed cooked chicken**
1¾ cups **frozen French-style green beans**
1 can (10¾ ounces) **condensed cream of mushroom soup, undiluted**
1 can (10¾ ounces) **condensed cream of chicken and broccoli soup, undiluted**
1 can (4 ounces) **mushroom stems and pieces, drained**
⅔ cup **chopped onion**
⅔ cup **chopped green pepper**
1 envelope **onion soup mix**
¾ cup **shredded Colby cheese**

ADDITIONAL INGREDIENT (for each casserole):
   ⅔ cup **french-fried onions**

Prepare wild rice according to package directions. Stir in chicken, beans, soups, mushrooms, onion, green pepper and soup mix. Spoon into two greased 1½-qt. baking dishes. Sprinkle with cheese. Cover and freeze one casserole for up to 3 months. Cover and bake the second casserole at 350° for 25–30 minutes or until heated through. Uncover and sprinkle with french-fried onions; bake 5 minutes longer or until onions are golden. **To use frozen casserole:** Completely thaw in the refrigerator. Remove from the refrigerator 30 minutes before baking. Cover and bake at 350° for 60–65 minutes or until heated through. Uncover and sprinkle with french-fried onions; bake 5 minutes longer. **Yield:** 2 casseroles (4–6 servings each).

Catch-of-the-Day Fish

Anglers will be hooked on this clever catch of the day, developed by the Taste of Home Test Kitchen. Simply dress up fillets with cheesy "scales" (scalloped potatoes from a package). Lemon slices and lime wedges do double duty, adding fun finishing touches and refreshing flavor when squeezed over the fish.

1 package (5 ounces) cheesy scalloped potatoes with skins
4 fresh *or* frozen fish fillets (about 1 pound), thawed
16 lime wedges
2 lemon slices, halved
4 ripe olive slices
8 pimiento pieces

Prepare scalloped potatoes, following the package directions for stovetop method. Place fish in an ungreased 13-in. × 9-in. × 2-in. baking dish. Using tongs, arrange potatoes on fish to look like scales (see photo). Cover and bake at 450° for 8–10 minutes or until the fish flakes easily with a fork. Carefully transfer to serving plates. Garnish with lime for tails and fins, lemon for heads, olives for eyes, and pimientos for eyes and mouth. **Yield:** 4 servings.

Chicken Stew Over Biscuits

A pleasant sauce coats this chicken-and-veggie dinner that's slow-cooked to tender perfection, then served over biscuits. "When I first came up with this dish, my 2-year-old couldn't get enough of it," comments Kathy Garrett of Browns Mills, New Jersey.

2 envelopes chicken gravy mix
2 cups water
¾ cup white wine *or* chicken broth
2 garlic cloves, minced
1 tablespoon minced fresh parsley
1–2 teaspoons chicken bouillon granules
½ teaspoon pepper
5 medium carrots, cut into 1-inch chunks
1 large onion, cut into eight wedges
1 broiler/fryer chicken (3 to 4 pounds), cut up
3 tablespoons all-purpose flour
⅓ cup cold water
1 tube (7½ ounces) refrigerated buttermilk biscuits

In a slow cooker, combine gravy mix, water, wine or broth, garlic, parsley, bouillon and pepper until blended. Add the carrots, onion and chicken. Cover and cook on low for 7–8 hours. Increase heat to high. In a small bowl, combine the flour and cold water until smooth; gradually stir into slow cooker. Cover and cook for 1 hour. Meanwhile, bake biscuits according to package directions. Place biscuits in soup bowls; top with stew. **Yield:** 4–6 servings.

Bavarian Sausage Supper

"My mom, who's a great cook, shared the recipe for this easy skillet meal," comments Pat Frankovich of North Olmsted, Ohio. *"Spicy kielbasa makes a flavored noodle and sauce mix truly delicious."*

> 2 cups coleslaw mix
> 1 cup thinly sliced carrots
> 2 tablespoons butter
> 2¼ cups water
> ¾ pound fully cooked kielbasa *or* Polish sausage, sliced
> 1 package (4½ ounces) quick-cooking noodles and sour cream chive sauce mix
> ½ teaspoon caraway seeds, optional

In a skillet, saute coleslaw mix and carrots in butter until crisp-tender. Add water; bring to a boil. Stir in remaining ingredients. Return to a boil; cook for 8 minutes or until noodles are tender, stirring occasionally. **Yield:** 5 servings.

Hearty Hamburger Casserole

"I love to invent my own recipes," relates Regan Delp of Independence, Virginia. *"I used convenient stuffing mix and canned vegetable soup to come up with this tasty and satisfying supper."*

> 1 pound ground beef
> 1 can (19 ounces) ready-to-serve chunky vegetable soup
> 1 package (6 ounces) instant stuffing mix
> ½ cup shredded cheddar cheese

In a skillet, cook beef until no longer pink; drain. Stir in soup and set aside. Prepare stuffing mix according to package directions; spoon half into a greased 2-qt. baking dish. Top with beef mixture, cheese and remaining stuffing. Bake, uncovered, at 350° for 30–35 minutes or until heated through. **Yield:** 4 servings.

Pork and Cabbage Dinner

Says Trina Hinkel of Minneapolis, Minnesota, "I put on this pork roast in the morning to avoid that evening dinner rush. All I do is fix potatoes, and our family can sit down to a satisfying supper."

1 pound carrots
1½ cups water
1 envelope onion soup mix
2 garlic cloves, minced
½ teaspoon celery seed
1 boneless pork shoulder roast (4 to 6 pounds)
½ teaspoon salt
¼ teaspoon pepper
1½ pounds cabbage, cut into 2-inch pieces

Cut carrots in half lengthwise and then into 2-in. pieces. Place in a 5-qt. slow cooker. Add water, soup mix, garlic and celery seed. Cut roast in half; place over carrot mixture. Sprinkle with salt and pepper. Cover and cook on high for 2 hours. Reduce heat to low; cook for 4 hours. Add cabbage; cook 2 hours longer or until the cabbage is tender and a meat thermometer reads 160°. Remove meat and vegetables to a serving plate; keep warm. If desired, thicken pan drippings for gravy and serve with the roast. **Yield:** 8–10 servings.

Meat Bun Bake

A meat bun is a golden, tender yeast roll filled with a mixture of cooked ground beef, cabbage and cheddar cheese. This casserole, from the Taste of Home Test Kitchen, captures the delicious flavor of the original in less than half the time.

1½ pounds ground beef
2 cups chopped cabbage
¼ cup chopped onion
½ teaspoon salt
¼ teaspoon pepper
1 cup shredded cheddar cheese
1½ cups biscuit/baking mix
1 cup milk
2 eggs

In a skillet, brown beef; drain. Add cabbage, onion, salt and pepper; cook over medium heat for 15 minutes or until the cabbage and onion are tender. Stir in cheese. Spoon into a greased 13-in. × 9-in. × 2-in. baking dish. In a bowl, blend biscuit mix, milk and eggs. Pour over beef mixture. Bake, uncovered, at 400° for 20–25 minutes or until golden brown. **Yield:** 6 servings.

Salmon Pasta Primavera

"I created this recipe one Sunday afternoon to use up ingredients I had on hand," comments Jenny Kimberlin of Overland Park, Kansas. *"My husband and a guest loved the tasty combination of salmon, vegetables and noodles."*

8 ounces uncooked spinach fettuccine, broken in half
1½ cups fresh *or* frozen broccoli florets
¼ cup chopped red onion
2 tablespoons chopped green pepper
2 garlic cloves, minced
4 tablespoons butter, *divided*
1 envelope Alfredo sauce mix
½ cup evaporated milk
½ cup water
Salt and pepper to taste
1 cup cubed cooked salmon
Crumbled cooked bacon, optional

Cook fettuccine according to package directions. Meanwhile, in a large skillet, saute the broccoli, onion, green pepper and garlic in 2 tablespoons butter until vegetables are tender. In a large saucepan, combine the sauce mix, milk, water, salt, pepper and remaining butter. Cook over medium heat until thickened. Add the salmon and heat through. Drain pasta; add to vegetable mixture. Top with sauce and gently toss to coat. Sprinkle with bacon if desired. **Yield:** 4 servings.

Crumb-Coated Cod

Fish fillets get fast flavor from Italian salad dressing mix and a breading made with seasoned stuffing mix. "I serve this baked fish with a tossed salad or relishes," remarks Julia Bruce of Tuscola, Illinois.

2 tablespoons vegetable oil
2 tablespoons water
1 envelope Italian salad dressing mix
2 cups crushed stuffing mix
4 cod fillets (about 6 ounces *each*)

In a shallow bowl, combine the oil, water and salad dressing mix. Place the stuffing mix in another bowl. Dip fillets in salad dressing mixture, then in stuffing. Place on a greased baking sheet. Bake at 425° for 15–20 minutes or until fish flakes easily with a fork. **Yield:** 4 servings.

Miniature Meat Pies

Gayle Lewis of Yucaipa, California shared the recipe for these cute little bites of flaky dough stuffed with an easy-to-season ground beef mixture. They're filling and oh-so-good served with ketchup.

1 pound ground beef
½ cup chili sauce
1 envelope onion soup mix
¼ teaspoon salt

DOUGH:
3 cups all-purpose flour
1–2 tablespoons sesame seeds, optional
1¼ teaspoons salt
1 cup shortening
¾ cup shredded cheddar cheese
¾ cup evaporated milk
1 tablespoon cider vinegar

In a skillet over medium heat, cook beef until no longer pink; drain. Stir in chili sauce, soup mix and salt; set aside. In a bowl, combine flour, sesame seeds if desired and salt. Cut in shortening and cheese until crumbly. Combine milk and vinegar; gradually add to flour mixture, tossing with a fork until dough forms a ball. Divide dough in half; roll out to ⅛-in. thickness. Cut with a 2½-in. round cutter. Place half of the circles 2 in. apart on ungreased baking sheets. Top each with about 1½ tablespoons of beef mixture; cover with remaining circles. Moisten edges with water and press with a fork to seal. Cut a slit in the top of each. Bake at 425° for 12–16 minutes or until golden brown. Serve immediately; or cool, wrap and freeze for up to 3 months. **Yield:** about 1½ dozen. **To use frozen meat pies:** Place on an ungreased baking sheet. Bake at 425° for 14–16 minutes or until heated through.

Macaroni Tuna Casserole

"This dish is so easy to fix, and the flavor is better than any tuna helper I've ever tried," says Suzanne Zick of Osceola, Arkansas. *"It was a staple when I was in college, because a box of macaroni and cheese and a can of tuna cost so little."*

1 package (7¼ ounces) macaroni and cheese
1 can (10¾ ounces) condensed cream of celery soup, undiluted
1 can (6 ounces) tuna, drained and flaked
½ cup milk
1 cup (4 ounces) shredded cheddar cheese
Minced fresh parsley, optional

Prepare macaroni and cheese according to package directions. Stir in soup, tuna and milk. Pour into a greased 2-qt. baking dish. Sprinkle with cheese and parsley if desired. Bake, uncovered, at 350° for 20 minutes or until cheese is melted. **Yield:** 4 servings.

Hot Hoagies

A convenient package of Italian salad dressing mix provides the yummy herb flavor in these broiled sandwiches that Paula Hadley assembles for her family of 10. "I use their favorite combination of meats and cheeses, then serve the sandwiches with chips and pickles," relates the Forest Hill, Louisiana cook. "They're a hit every time."

¾ cup butter, softened
1 envelope Italian salad dressing mix
6 hoagie buns, split
12–16 ounces sliced luncheon meat (salami, ham *and/or* turkey)
12 thin slices cheese (Swiss, cheddar *and/or* brick)

Combine butter and salad dressing mix; spread 1 tablespoonful inside each bun. On bottom of each bun, layer one slice of meat, two slices of cheese and another slice of meat; replace tops. Spread 1 tablespoon butter mixture over top of each bun. Place on a baking sheet. Broil 6 in. from the heat for 2–3 minutes or until tops are lightly browned. **Yield:** 6 servings.

Pork Chops with Apples and Stuffing

The heartwarming taste of cinnamon and apples is the perfect accompaniment to these tender pork chops. "This dish is always a winner with my family," notes Joan Hamilton of Worcester, Massachusetts. "Because it calls for only four ingredients, it's a main course I can serve with little preparation."

6 boneless pork loin chops (1 inch thick)
1 tablespoon vegetable oil
1 package (6 ounces) crushed stuffing mix
1 can (21 ounces) apple pie filling with cinnamon

In a skillet, brown pork chops in oil over medium-high heat. Meanwhile, prepare stuffing according to package directions. Spread pie filling into a greased 13-in. × 9-in. × 2-in. baking dish. Place the pork chops on top; spoon stuffing over chops. Cover and bake at 350° for 35 minutes. Uncover; bake 10 minutes longer or until a meat thermometer reads 160°. **Yield:** 6 servings.

Beefy Hash Brown Bake

A topping of french-fried onions provides a little crunch to this meaty main dish from Rochelle Boucher of Brooklyn, Wisconsin. "Since this casserole is practically a meal in itself, I simply accompany it with a fruit salad and dessert," she relates.

4 cups frozen shredded hash brown potatoes
3 tablespoons vegetable oil
⅛ teaspoon pepper
1 pound ground beef
1 cup water
1 envelope brown gravy mix
½ teaspoon garlic salt
2 cups frozen mixed vegetables
1 can (2.8 ounces) french-fried onions, *divided*
1 cup (4 ounces) shredded cheddar cheese, *divided*

In a bowl, combine the potatoes, oil and pepper. Press into a greased 8-in. square baking dish. Bake, uncovered, at 350° for 15–20 minutes or until potatoes are thawed and set. Meanwhile, in a saucepan over medium heat, cook the beef until no longer pink; drain. Stir in water, gravy mix and garlic salt. Bring to a boil; cook and stir for 2 minutes. Add vegetables; cook and stir for 5 minutes. Stir in half of the onions and cheese. Pour over potatoes. Bake for 5–10 minutes. Sprinkle with remaining onions and cheese; bake 5 minutes longer or until cheese is melted. **Yield:** 4 servings.

Taco-Filled Pasta Shells

2 pounds ground beef
2 envelopes taco seasoning
1 package (8 ounces) cream cheese, cubed
24 uncooked jumbo pasta shells
¼ cup butter, melted
ADDITIONAL INGREDIENTS (for each casserole):
1 cup salsa
1 cup taco sauce
1 cup (4 ounces) shredded cheddar cheese
1 cup (4 ounces) shredded Monterey Jack *or* mozzarella cheese
1½ cups crushed tortilla chips
1 cup (8 ounces) sour cream
3 green onions, chopped

"I've been stuffing pasta shells with different fillings for years, but my family enjoys this version with taco-seasoned meat the most," says Marge Hodel of Roanoke, Illinois. "The frozen shells are so convenient, because you can take out only the number you need for a single-serving lunch or family dinner. Just add zippy taco sauce and bake."

In a skillet, cook beef until no longer pink; drain. Add taco seasoning; prepare according to package directions. Add cream cheese; cover and simmer for 5–10 minutes or until melted. Transfer to a bowl; chill for 1 hour. Cook pasta according to package directions; drain. Gently toss with butter. Fill each shell with about 3 tablespoons meat mixture. Place 12 shells in a greased 9-in. square baking dish. Cover and freeze for up to 3 months. To prepare remaining shells, spoon salsa into a greased 9-in. square baking dish. Top with stuffed shells and taco sauce. Cover and bake at 350° for 30 minutes. Uncover; sprinkle with cheeses and chips. Bake 15 minutes longer or until heated through. Serve with sour cream and onions. **To use frozen shells:** Thaw in the refrigerator for 24 hours (shells will be partially frozen). Remove from dish. Add salsa to dish; top with shells and taco sauce. Cover and bake at 350° for 40 minutes. Uncover; continue as above. **Yield:** 2 casseroles (6 servings each).

Chicken Ranch Potatoes

Top hot potatoes with this colorful mixture from Edie Despain of Logan, Utah for a satisfying meal. "You'll get rave reviews on this one," Edie promises. "Quick to prepare, it's also delicious. Ranch salad dressing is a tasty change from the usual sour cream," she adds.

2½ cups cubed cooked chicken
1 package (10 ounces) frozen mixed vegetables
Salt and pepper to taste
¾ cup ranch salad dressing
4 hot baked potatoes

Place chicken and vegetables in a 2-qt. microwave-safe dish; cover and microwave on high for 6–7 minutes, stirring once. Add salt and pepper. Let stand for 2 minutes. Fold in salad dressing. With a sharp knife, cut an X in the top of each potato; fluff pulp with a fork. Top with chicken mixture. **Yield:** 4 servings.

Tex-Mex Pitas

"I sometimes treat my friends at work to these peppy pitas at lunchtime," relates Helen Overman of Pottsboro, Texas. "I prepare everything in advance, so the spicy sandwiches can just be zapped in the microwave."

2 pounds ground beef
1 envelope taco seasoning
⅓ cup water
1 can (16 ounces) refried beans
1 can (10 ounces) diced tomatoes and green chilies, undrained
Pinch ground cumin
7 pita breads (6 inches), halved
3 cups (12 ounces) shredded cheddar cheese
Sliced jalapenos

In a skillet, cook beef over medium heat until no longer pink; drain. Stir in taco seasoning, water, beans, tomatoes and cumin. Simmer, uncovered, for 20 minutes, stirring occasionally. Spoon about ⅓ cup into each pita half; top with about 2 tablespoons cheese and a few jalapeno slices. Place in an ungreased 13-in. × 9-in. × 2-in. baking pan. Bake at 350° for 10 minutes or until cheese is melted. **Yield:** 7 servings.

Au Gratin Sausage Skillet

"Using frozen vegetables and a package of au gratin potatoes, I can get this satisfying stovetop supper on the table in no time," reports Penny Greene of Lancaster, Ohio. *"Even our oldest daughter, who can be a picky eater, loves it— and it is an excellent way of getting her to eat her vegetables."*

1 pound fully cooked kielbasa *or* Polish sausage, halved and sliced ½ inch thick
2 tablespoons vegetable oil
1 package (5¼ ounces) au gratin potatoes
2½ cups water
1 package (8 ounces) frozen California blend vegetables
1–2 cups (4 to 8 ounces) shredded cheddar cheese

In a skillet, cook sausage in oil until lightly browned; drain. Add potatoes with contents of sauce mix and water. Cover and cook over medium heat for 18–20 minutes or until the potatoes are almost tender, stirring occasionally. Add vegetables; cover and cook for 8–10 minutes or until potatoes and vegetables are tender. Sprinkle with cheese. Remove from the heat; cover and let stand for 2 minutes or until the cheese is melted. **Yield:** 4 servings.

Editor's Note: The milk and butter listed on the potato package are not used in this recipe.

Beefy Rice Dinner

In Bay City, Texas, Mildred Sherrer turns a boxed rice mix into a complete meal by adding ground beef, celery and green pepper. "It's so quick to fix and makes a flavorful, filling main dish," she notes.

1 package (6.8 ounces) beef-flavored rice mix
½ pound lean ground beef
⅓ cup chopped celery
⅓ cup chopped green pepper
⅛–¼ teaspoon salt
⅛ teaspoon pepper
⅓ cup shredded cheddar cheese

Prepare rice according to package directions. Meanwhile, in a large skillet, cook beef, celery and green pepper until the meat is browned and vegetables are tender; drain. Add rice, salt and pepper. Transfer to a greased 2-qt. baking dish. Sprinkle with cheese. Bake, uncovered, at 350° for 10–15 minutes or until heated through and cheese is melted. **Yield:** 4–6 servings.

Peppy Macaroni

"I like to keep an extra box of macaroni and cheese on the pantry shelf to make this fun pizza-flavored casserole for unexpected guests," relates Helen Cluts of Sioux Falls, South Dakota. It's a snap to prepare, so older kids could assemble it.

1 package (7¼ ounces) macaroni and cheese dinner
2 eggs, lightly beaten
1 jar (8 ounces) pizza sauce
40 slices pepperoni (about 2½ ounces)
2 cups (8 ounces) shredded mozzarella cheese

Prepare macaroni and cheese according to package directions. Fold in eggs. Spread into a greased 13-in. × 9-in. × 2-in. baking dish. Top with pizza sauce, pepperoni and mozzarella. Bake, uncovered, at 350° for 30–35 minutes or until lightly browned and cheese is melted. Let stand for 5 minutes before serving. **Yield:** 4 servings.

Cube Steaks with Gravy

"Before I tried this recipe, my family did not like this particular cut of beef because it was chewy. But these cube steaks, slow-cooked until they're nice and tender, are now one of our favorites," Judy Long of Limestone, Tennessee reports. "Since we love mushrooms, I often add a can of them to the gravy."

⅓ cup all-purpose flour
6 beef cube steaks (1½ pounds)
1 tablespoon vegetable oil
1 large onion, sliced and separated into rings
3 cups water, *divided*
1 envelope brown gravy mix
1 envelope mushroom gravy mix
1 envelope onion gravy mix
Hot mashed potatoes *or* cooked noodles

Place flour in a large resealable plastic bag. Add steaks, a few at a time, and shake until completely coated. In a skillet, cook steaks in oil until lightly browned on each side. Transfer to a slow cooker. Add the onion and 2 cups water. Cover and cook on low for 8 hours or until meat is  tender. In a bowl, whisk together gravy mixes with remaining water. Add to slow cooker; cook 30 minutes longer. Serve over mashed potatoes or noodles. **Yield:** 6 servings.

Ham 'n' Noodle Toss

"My family likes ramen noodles, so I'm always looking for new ways to use them," notes Margaret Pache of Mesa, Arizona. *"This satisfying supper is a much-requested favorite."*

2 cups broccoli florets
1¾ cups water
1¼ cups cubed fully cooked ham
1 tablespoon soy sauce
2 packages (3 ounces *each*) oriental-flavored ramen noodles
Sliced ripe olives, optional

In a large saucepan, combine broccoli, water, ham, soy sauce and one flavoring packet from the noodles (discard second packet or save for another use). Break noodles into small pieces; add to pan. Simmer, uncovered, for 6–8 minutes or until noodles are tender, stirring frequently. Top with olives if desired. **Yield:** 4 servings.

Beef and Tomato Pie

"I bake this hot and hearty ground beef pie when my grandchildren come to visit," comments June Mullins of Livonia, Missouri. *"They like its family-pleasing flavor."*

1 pound ground beef
1 large onion, chopped
2 tablespoons ketchup
½ teaspoon salt
2 cups biscuit/baking mix
⅔ cup milk
1 cup diced fresh tomato
½ cup shredded cheddar cheese

In a skillet over medium heat, cook beef and onion until meat is no longer pink; drain. Remove from the heat. Stir in ketchup and salt; set aside. Combine biscuit mix and

milk just until moistened. Turn onto a lightly floured surface and knead 6–8 times. Roll into a 10-in. circle; transfer to a greased 9-in. pie plate. Flute edges. Spoon meat mixture into crust. Sprinkle with tomatoes. Bake at 425° for 20–25 minutes. Sprinkle with cheese; bake 2 minutes longer or until cheese is melted. **Yield:** 6 servings.

Mexicali Pork Chops

You'll need just four ingredients to fix these tender pork chops from Laura Cohen of Eau Claire, Wisconsin. They get their zippy flavor from a packet of taco seasoning and salsa.

1 envelope taco seasoning
4 boneless pork loin chops (½ inch thick)
1 tablespoon vegetable oil
Salsa

Rub taco seasoning over pork chops. In a skillet, cook chops in oil over medium-high heat until meat is no longer pink and juices run clear, about 9 minutes. Serve with salsa. **Yield:** 4 servings.

Swift Spaghetti

Louise Miller of West-minster, Maryland adds dry onion soup mix to the water when cooking her spaghetti, then stirs in a nicely seasoned meat sauce. "This dish has so much flavor that I'm always asked for the recipe," she notes.

5½ cups water
1 package (7 ounces) spaghetti
1 envelope onion soup mix
1 pound ground beef
1 can (8 ounces) tomato sauce
1 can (6 ounces) tomato paste
1 tablespoon dried parsley flakes
1 teaspoon dried oregano
½ teaspoon dried basil
¼–½ teaspoon garlic powder

In a large saucepan, bring water to a boil. Add spaghetti and soup mix. Cook for 12–15 minutes or until spaghetti is tender (do not drain). Meanwhile, in a skillet, cook beef over medium heat until no longer pink; drain. Stir in the tomato sauce, tomato paste, parsley, oregano, basil and garlic powder. Add to the spaghetti mixture; heat through. **Yield:** 4–6 servings.

Spicy Jambalaya

In Eufaula, Alabama, Amy Chop uses just the right amount of seasonings to spice up this memorable main dish. It's loaded with zesty sausage, tender chicken and tasty shrimp, too.

1 package (4.4 ounces) chicken-flavored rice and sauce mix
½ pound boneless skinless chicken breasts, cubed
¼ pound bulk Italian sausage
2 garlic cloves, minced
2 tablespoons butter
1 medium green pepper, chopped
1 celery rib, thinly sliced
1 small onion, chopped
1 medium tomato, chopped
½–1 teaspoon ground cumin
½ teaspoon dried oregano
½ teaspoon salt
½ teaspoon pepper
⅛ teaspoon hot pepper sauce
¼ pound uncooked medium shrimp, peeled, deveined and chopped

Prepare rice mix according to package directions. Meanwhile, in a large skillet, cook chicken, sausage and garlic in butter for 5 minutes. Add the green pepper, celery and onion; cook and stir until meat is no longer pink and vegetables are tender. Stir in tomato and seasonings; heat through. Add the shrimp; cook and stir for 3–4 minutes or until shrimp turn pink. Serve with the prepared rice. **Yield:** 4 servings.

Rice Mix Meatballs

"Mom often prepared these easy meatballs with a thick gravy when I was growing up," relates Marcy Paden of Louisville, Nebraska. "Now I make them for my family as a nice change of pace from hamburgers." With just five ingredients, they're a snap to whip up.

1 package (6.8 ounces) beef-flavored rice mix
1 egg, beaten
1 pound ground beef
2½ cups boiling water
2 tablespoons cornstarch
3 tablespoons cold water

Set contents of rice seasoning packet aside. In a bowl, combine the rice and egg. Add beef and mix well. Shape into 1-in. balls. In a large skillet over medium heat, brown the meatballs on all sides. Meanwhile, in a small bowl, combine reserved seasoning packet and boiling water. Add to skillet; cover and simmer for 30 minutes or until the rice is tender. Combine cornstarch and cold water until smooth; add to skillet. Bring to a boil. Cook and stir for 2 minutes or until thickened. **Yield:** 8–10 servings.

Green Pepper Meat Loaf

"My husband, Wayne, asks for this meat loaf all the time," reports Edna Lauderdale of Milwaukee, Wisconsin. "We like it spicy, so we use hot sausage rather than mild. Slices are terrific drizzled with ketchup, served with mashed potatoes and gravy, or in meat loaf sandwiches the next day."

2 eggs, lightly beaten
2 medium green peppers, chopped
1 large onion, finely chopped
¼ cup chopped celery leaves
¼ cup minced fresh parsley
1 envelope onion soup mix
2 pounds ground beef
1 pound bulk pork sausage
4 bacon strips, optional

In a large bowl, combine eggs, green peppers, onion, celery leaves, parsley and soup mix. Crumble beef and sausage over the mixture and mix well. Shape into a 12-in. × 4-in. loaf. Place on a rack in a shallow baking pan. Bake, uncovered, at 350° for 1 hour. Place bacon strips over top if desired. Bake 45–60 minutes longer or until no pink remains and a meat thermometer reads 160°. **Yield:** 14 slices.

Herbed Shrimp Fettuccine

"Everyone will think you went all out when you serve this impressive seafood entree," promises Marilyn Weaver of Sparks, Maryland. *"You'll be amazed, though, at how easy and quick it is to fix."*

6 ounces fettuccine *or* medium egg noodles
1 envelope herb and garlic soup mix
1¾ cups milk
1 pound uncooked shrimp, peeled and deveined
2 cups broccoli florets
¼ cup grated Parmesan cheese

Cook fettuccine according to package directions. Meanwhile, combine soup mix and milk in a saucepan. Cook and stir over medium heat until smooth. Add shrimp and broccoli; simmer, uncovered, for 3–5 minutes or until shrimp are pink (do not boil). Drain pasta; toss with the shrimp mixture. Sprinkle with Parmesan cheese. **Yield:** 4 servings.

No-Fuss Meat Loaf

"Instant stuffing mix makes this meat loaf simple enough for beginners to make," says Betty Braswell of Elgin, Pennsylvania. *"Combine the mixture in a resealable plastic bag instead of a bowl, then I toss the bag for easy cleanup."*

2 eggs
½ cup water
1 package (6 ounces) instant stuffing mix
2 pounds ground beef
Ketchup

In a large bowl, beat eggs and water. Add stuffing mix and contents of seasoning packet; mix well. Add beef; mix well. Press into an ungreased 9-in. × 5-in. × 3-in. loaf pan. Top with ketchup. Bake, uncovered, at 350° for 1¼ to 1½ hours or until no pink remains and a meat thermometer reads 160°. **Yield:** 6–8 servings.

Piggies in Blankies

Iola Egle of McCook, Nebraska presents a pretty platter of franks nestled in sauerkraut and wrapped in tender biscuit blankets. They're easy to assemble and a cinch to make.

2 cups biscuit/baking mix
½ cup water
1 can (14 ounces) sauerkraut, rinsed and drained, *divided*
1 pound hot dogs

In a bowl, combine biscuit mix and water until a soft dough forms. Turn onto a floured surface; knead 5–10 times. Roll dough into a 13-in. circle; cut into 10 wedges. Place 1 tablespoon sauerkraut on each wedge. Place a hot dog at the wide end; roll up each wedge tightly. Place on an ungreased baking sheet. Bake at 450° for 12–15 minutes or until golden brown. Heat remaining sauerkraut; serve with the hot dogs. **Yield:** 10 servings.

Scalloped Potatoes with Ham

"I fix this saucy skillet dish often, especially when I'm running late, because it takes so little time to prepare," reports Emma Magielda of Amsterdam, New York. "The recipe won first prize in our local paper some years back."

4 medium potatoes, peeled and thinly sliced
2 tablespoons butter
⅓ cup water
½ cup milk
2–3 tablespoons onion soup mix
3 tablespoons minced fresh parsley
1 cup cubed process American cheese
1 cup cubed fully cooked ham

In a large skillet, cook potatoes in butter until potatoes are evenly coated. Add water; bring to a boil. Reduce heat; cover and simmer for 14 minutes or until potatoes are tender. In a bowl, combine the milk, dry soup mix and parsley; stir in cheese. Pour over potatoes. Add ham; cook and stir gently until cheese is melted and sauce is smooth. Serve immediately. **Yield:** 4 servings.

Italian Beef Hoagies

You'll need just five ingredients to feed a crowd these tender tangy sandwiches. "On weekends, I start the roast the night before, so I can shred it in the morning," says Lori Piatt of Danville, Illinois.

  1 boneless sirloin tip roast (about 4 pounds), halved
  2 envelopes Italian salad dressing mix
  2 cups water
  1 jar (16 ounces) mild pepper rings, undrained
18 hoagie buns, split

Place roast in a 5-qt. slow cooker. Combine the salad dressing mix and water; pour over roast. Cover and cook on low for 8 hours or until meat is tender. Remove meat; shred with a fork and return to slow cooker. Add pepper rings; heat through. Spoon ½ cup meat mixture onto each bun. **Yield:** 18 servings.

Three-Step Stir-Fry

"I based this flavorful stir-fry on a fabulous dish I sampled in a San Francisco restaurant," notes Amy Masson of Cypress, California. "It truly is a 10-minute main dish that looks and tastes like it took a lot longer."

1 envelope stir-fry seasoning mix
1 package (16 ounces) broccoli coleslaw
2 tablespoons vegetable oil
8 ounces thinly sliced roast beef *or* other deli meat, cut into ½-inch strips
1 can (8 ounces) sliced water chestnuts, drained
3 plum tomatoes, quartered
2 teaspoons sesame seeds

Prepare seasoning mix according to package directions; set aside. In a skillet, stir-fry coleslaw in oil for 3 minutes or until crisp-tender. Add beef, water chestnuts, tomatoes, sesame seeds and seasoning sauce. Cook 4 minutes longer or until heated through. **Yield:** 7 servings.

Pantry Skillet

An envelope of soup mix gives fast flavor to this beefy stovetop supper by Susie Smith of Sauk Village, Illinois. "I came up with this all-in-one dish by using whatever ingredients I had on hand," she explains.

1 pound ground beef
1 can (10¾ ounces) condensed tomato soup, undiluted
1½ cups water
1 envelope onion mushroom soup mix
½ pound fresh mushrooms, sliced
1½ cups frozen cut green beans
3 medium carrots, grated
1 cup cooked rice
2 slices process American cheese, cut into strips

In a large skillet over medium heat, cook beef until no longer pink; drain. Stir in the soup, water and soup mix; mix well. Stir in mushrooms, beans, carrots and rice. Bring to a boil. Reduce heat; cover and simmer for 5–7 minutes or until beans are tender. Top with cheese; cover and let stand until cheese is melted. **Yield:** 6 servings.

Fiesta Fry Pan Dinner

Taco seasoning mix adds fast flavor to this speedy skillet dish from Leota Shaffer. "It's so easy to make that I fix it frequently," says the Sterling, Virginia, cook. "All I need is salad and dessert, and the meal is ready."

1 pound ground turkey *or* beef
½ cup chopped onion
1 envelope taco seasoning
1½ cups water
1½ cups sliced zucchini
1 can (14½ ounces) stewed tomatoes, undrained
1 cup frozen corn
1½ cups uncooked instant rice
1 cup (4 ounces) shredded cheddar cheese

In a skillet, cook turkey and onion until meat is no longer pink; drain if necessary. Stir in taco seasoning, water, zucchini, tomatoes and corn; bring to a boil. Add rice. Reduce heat; cover and simmer for 5 minutes or until rice is tender and liquid is absorbed. Sprinkle with cheese; cover and let stand until the cheese is melted. **Yield:** 8-10 servings.

Flavorful Swedish Meatballs

"Our kids—Garrett and Heather—love to roll the ground beef and pork mixture into these moist meatballs," says Stacy Thomas of Anchorage, Alaska. "We enjoy them prepared in a creamy gravy. But the frozen meatballs also are great additions to soups and stews, or to stir into spaghetti sauce and serve over pasta."

2 eggs, lightly beaten
¼ cup ketchup
¾ cup dry bread crumbs
2 tablespoons dried parsley flakes
2 tablespoons Worcestershire sauce
1 teaspoon onion powder
1 teaspoon garlic powder
1 teaspoon pepper
½ teaspoon salt
½ teaspoon chili powder
2 pounds ground beef
1 pound ground pork

ADDITIONAL INGREDIENTS (for each batch):
1 envelope brown gravy mix
½ cup sour cream
Dash *each* nutmeg and pepper
Hot cooked noodles

In a bowl, combine the first 10 ingredients. Crumble meat over mixture and mix well. Shape into 1-in. balls (about 6 dozen). Place in a single layer in ungreased 15-in. × 10-in. × 1-in. baking pans. Bake at 400° for 20 minutes or until no longer pink, turning often. Cool. Place about 35 meatballs each into freezer containers. May be frozen for up to 3 months. **Yield:** 2 batches (35 meatballs per batch). **To prepare Swedish meatballs:** Completely thaw in the refrigerator. In a large skillet, prepare gravy according to package directions. Add meatballs; cover and cook for 10 minutes or until heated through. Remove from the heat; stir in the sour cream, nutmeg and pepper. Serve over noodles. **Yield:** 7 servings.

Franks and Corn Bread

"We ate this corn bread-topped casserole often when our children were growing up, and it was always well received," shares Marilyn Hoiten of Rockford, Illinois. *"It's so easy to throw together after work that I still make it for my husband and me."*

2 cans (16 ounces *each*) pork and beans
1 package (12 ounces) hot dogs, halved lengthwise and sliced
2 tablespoons brown sugar
2 tablespoons Worcestershire sauce
2 tablespoons prepared mustard
1 package (8½ ounces) corn bread/muffin mix
1 cup (4 ounces) shredded cheddar cheese

In a bowl, combine the first five ingredients; mix well. Transfer to a greased 9-in. square baking dish. Prepare corn bread batter according to package directions; stir in cheese. Drop by spoonfuls onto bean mixture. Bake, uncovered, at 350° for 40–45 minutes or until heated through. **Yield:** 6 servings.

Italian Chicken and Rice

"I combined the best of three favorite recipes to come up with this tender and tasty chicken-rice combination," says Cathee Bethel of Lebanon, Oregon. *"It's my family's favorite way to eat chicken."*

⅔ cup biscuit/baking mix
⅓ cup grated Parmesan cheese
2 teaspoons Italian seasoning
1 teaspoon paprika
1 can (5 ounces) evaporated milk, *divided*
6 boneless skinless chicken breast halves
2 cups boiling water
2 cups uncooked instant rice
1 teaspoon salt, optional
2 tablespoons butter, melted

In a large resealable plastic bag or shallow bowl, combine the first four ingredients. Place ⅓ cup milk in another bowl. Dip chicken in milk, then coat with the cheese mixture. In a greased 13-in. × 9-in. × 2-in. baking dish, combine water, rice, salt if desired and remaining milk; mix well. Top with chicken. Drizzle with butter. Bake, uncovered, at 425° for 25–30 minutes or until the rice is tender and chicken juices run clear. **Yield:** 6 servings.

MAIN DISHES

Taco Pizza

Convenient prebaked crust makes this tasty taco pizza as easy as can be. "This is a great recipe, especially if you have teenagers," comments Mary Cass of Balto, Maryland. "I keep the ingredients on hand so that we can whip up this filling meal anytime."

1 pound ground beef
1 envelope taco seasoning
1 cup water
2 prebaked Italian bread shell crusts (12 inches)
1 can (16 ounces) refried beans
¾ cup salsa
2 cups coarsely crushed tortilla chips
2 cups (8 ounces) shredded cheddar cheese
2 medium tomatoes, chopped, optional
1 cup shredded lettuce, optional

In a saucepan, cook beef over medium heat until no longer pink; drain. Stir in taco seasoning and water. Bring to a boil; reduce heat. Simmer, uncovered, for 10 minutes; set aside. Place crusts on ungreased pizza pans or baking sheets. Combine beans and salsa; spread over crusts. Top with beef mixture, chips and cheese. Bake at 350° for 13–16 minutes or until cheese is melted. Sprinkle with tomatoes and lettuce if desired. **Yield:** 2 pizzas (6–8 servings each).

Meaty Mac 'n' Cheese

"My husband is disabled and requires constant care. This doesn't leave me a lot of time to cook, so I came up with this tasty way to beef up a box of macaroni and cheese," explains Charlotte Kremer of Pahrump, Nevada. The hearty mixture gets extra flavor from corn, ripe olives and zippy salsa.

1 package (7¼ ounces) macaroni and cheese
1 pound ground beef
¼ cup chopped onion
1½ cups salsa
½ cup fresh *or* frozen corn
1 can (2¼ ounces) sliced ripe olives, drained
3 tablespoons diced pimientos
Shredded cheddar cheese
Chopped tomato

Set aside cheese sauce mix from macaroni and cheese; cook macaroni according to package directions. Meanwhile, in a large saucepan, cook beef and onion until meat is no longer pink; drain. Add the salsa, corn, olives and pimientos; heat through. Drain macaroni; add to beef mixture with contents of cheese sauce mix. Mix well; heat through. Garnish with cheese and tomato. **Yield:** 4–6 servings. **Editor's Note:** The milk and butter listed on the macaroni and cheese package are not used in this recipe.

Turkey Burger Pie

"This recipe saved the day when I came home from the hospital after delivering our son," recalls Danielle Monai of Brooklyn Heights, Ohio. *"It requires just six ingredients and bakes in less than half an hour, so I can make dinner in a jiffy."*

1 pound ground turkey breast
1 cup chopped onion
1 cup reduced-fat shredded cheddar cheese
Egg substitute equivalent to 2 eggs
1 cup fat-free milk
½ cup reduced-fat biscuit/baking mix

In a skillet over medium heat, cook turkey and onion until meat is no longer pink; drain. Transfer to a 9-in. pie plate coated with nonstick cooking spray. Sprinkle with cheese. In a bowl, combine egg substitute, milk and baking mix; mix well. Pour over cheese. Bake at 400° for 20–25 minutes or until golden brown and a knife inserted near the center comes out clean. **Yield:** 6 servings.

Tamale Pie

"My whole family really enjoys Mexican food," remarks Nancy Roberts of Cave City, Arkansas. *"When I'm in a hurry, I make this zippy deep-dish pie. It always satisfies their appetites."*

1 pound ground beef
¼ pound bulk pork sausage
¼ cup chopped onion
1 garlic clove, minced
1 can (14½ ounces) stewed tomatoes, drained
1 can (11 ounces) whole kernel corn, drained
1 can (6 ounces) tomato paste
¼ cup sliced ripe olives
1½ teaspoons chili powder
½ teaspoon salt
1 egg
⅓ cup milk
1 package (8½ ounces) corn bread/muffin mix
Paprika
½ cup shredded cheddar cheese

In a 2½-qt. microwave-safe dish, combine beef, sausage, onion and garlic. Cover and microwave on high for 5–6 minutes, stirring once to crumble meat. Drain. Add the tomatoes, corn, tomato paste, olives, chili powder and salt; mix well. Cover and microwave on high for 6–8 minutes or until heated through. In a bowl, beat egg; add milk and corn bread mix. Stir just until moistened. Spoon over meat mixture; sprinkle with paprika. Microwave, uncovered, on high for 10–11 minutes or until a toothpick inserted near the center of the corn bread comes out clean. Sprinkle with cheese. **Yield:** 6 servings.

Corn in the Cobbler

Canned goods and corn bread mix combine in this golden bake from Judith Taylor of North Attleboro, Massachusetts. "When I served it to my parents, they loved it," she reports. "It makes a lot, so I often freeze half."

1 can (15 ounces) corned beef hash
2 cans (8 ounces *each*) tomato sauce
½ cup diced green pepper
2 tablespoons plus 1 teaspoon dried minced onion, *divided*
2 tablespoons Worcestershire sauce
½ teaspoon salt
¼ teaspoon pepper
1 package (8½ ounces) corn bread/muffin mix
1 cup all-purpose flour
1 cup milk
2 eggs, beaten
2 cups (8 ounces) shredded cheddar cheese, *divided*

In a large bowl, combine hash, tomato sauce, green pepper, 2 tablespoons onion, Worcestershire sauce, salt and pepper; set aside. In another bowl, combine the corn bread mix, flour, milk and eggs just until moistened. Add 1 cup cheese and remaining onion. Spread batter into a greased 13-in. × 9-in. × 2-in. baking dish. Spread hash mixture evenly over top. Sprinkle with remaining cheese. Bake, uncovered, at 375° for 35 minutes or until corn bread layer is golden brown and pulls away from the sides of the pan. **Yield:** 12–16 servings.

Artichoke Tuna Toss

"I do volunteer work one evening a week and leave a meal behind for my family," relates Emily Perez of Alexandria, Virginia. "On one occasion, I left this made-in-minutes medley. When I came home, my husband said it was the best pasta dish I'd ever fixed!"

3½ cups water
¼ cup butter
2 packages (4.6 ounces each) garlic and olive oil vermicelli mix
1 can (16 ounces) artichoke hearts, undrained and quartered
2 cans (6 ounces *each*) tuna, drained and flaked
1 package (10 ounces) frozen peas
1 tablespoon olive oil
1 tablespoon red wine vinegar
4–6 garlic cloves, minced

In a saucepan, bring water and butter to a boil. Stir in vermicelli with contents of seasoning packets, artichokes, tuna, peas, oil, vinegar and garlic. Return to a boil; cook, uncovered, for 8–10 minutes or until vermicelli is tender. Let stand 5 minutes before serving. **Yield:** 6 servings.

Shrimp Taco Salad

"I created this main-dish salad to satisfy our family's love of shrimp," says Ellen Morrell of Hazleton, Pennsylvania. *"It has lots of contrasting textures, including firm taco-seasoned shrimp, crispy tortilla strips and hearty black beans. A convenient bag of salad greens cuts down on prep time, so I can have this meal ready in half an hour."*

1 pound uncooked large shrimp, peeled and deveined
1 envelope taco seasoning, *divided*
½ cup plus 3 tablespoons olive oil, *divided*
1 small onion, finely chopped
3 tablespoons red wine vinegar
2 tablespoons diced green *or* sweet red pepper
6 garlic cloves, minced
½ teaspoon ground coriander
¼ teaspoon sugar
3 corn tortillas (6 inches), cut into ¼ inch strips
1 package (8 ounces) ready-to-serve salad greens
1 medium tomato, chopped
1 can (8 ounces) black beans, rinsed and drained
2 cups (8 ounces) finely shredded Colby/Monterey Jack cheese

Remove shrimp tails if desired. Place shrimp in a bowl; sprinkle with half of the taco seasoning. Set aside. In another bowl, combine ½ cup oil, onion, vinegar, green pepper, garlic, coriander and sugar; set aside. In a skillet, stir-fry tortilla strips in remaining oil; drain on paper towels. Sprinkle with remaining taco seasoning. In the same skillet, saute shrimp for 8–10 minutes or until pink. In a large bowl, combine the greens, tomato, beans, shrimp and tortilla strips. Drizzle with dressing. Sprinkle with cheese; toss. **Yield:** 6–8 servings.

Beef Veggie Casserole

"This satisfying stew is a breeze to fix because it uses leftover roast beef and refrigerated biscuits," promises Patti Keith of Ebensburg, Pennsylvania. "With hearty chunks of potato and plenty of mixed vegetables, it makes a wonderful meal with a loaf of garlic bread."

1 envelope mushroom gravy mix
¾ cup water
2 cups cubed cooked beef
2 cups frozen mixed vegetables, thawed
2 medium potatoes, peeled, cooked and cubed
1 tube (12 ounces) refrigerated buttermilk biscuits, separated into 10 biscuits

In a saucepan, combine gravy mix and water until smooth. Bring to a boil; cook and stir for 1 minute or until thickened. Stir in beef, mixed vegetables and potatoes; heat through. Transfer to a greased 8-in. square baking dish. Top with biscuits. Bake at 400° for 12–16 minutes or until biscuits are golden and meat mixture is bubbly. **Yield:** 5 servings.

Three-Step Stroganoff

"I think the less time it takes to prepare supper, the better," states Joyce Key of Snellville, Georgia. This fast version of traditional Beef Stroganoff is from a community cookbook my mother gave me."

1½ pounds boneless round steak, thinly sliced
1 tablespoon vegetable oil
1 can (10¾ ounces) condensed cream of mushroom soup, undiluted
½ cup water
1 envelope onion soup mix
½ cup sour cream
Hot cooked noodles
Minced fresh parsley, optional

In a large skillet, stir-fry beef in oil until no longer pink. Stir in soup, water and onion soup mix. Reduce heat; cover and simmer for 20 minutes. Stir in sour cream; heat through (do not boil). Serve over noodles; garnish with parsley if desired. **Yield:** 6 servings.

Sweet and Savory Brisket

"I like this recipe not only because it makes such tender and flavorful beef, but because it takes advantage of a slow cooker," explains Chris Snyder of Boulder, Colorado. "It's wonderful to come home from work and have this mouth-watering main dish waiting for you. The beef doubles as a warm sandwich filling, too."

    1 beef brisket (3 to 3½ pounds), cut in half
    1 cup ketchup
    ¼ cup grape jelly
    1 envelope onion soup mix
    ½ teaspoon pepper

Place half of the brisket in a slow cooker. In a bowl, combine the ketchup, jelly, dry soup mix and pepper; spread half over meat. Top with the remaining meat and ketchup mixture. Cover and cook on low for 8–10 hours or until meat is tender. Slice brisket; serve with cooking juices. **Yield:** 8–10 servings. **Editor's Note:** This is a fresh beef brisket, not corned beef.

Flip-Over Pizza

"Your family is sure to enjoy this easy pizza that you flip over before serving," notes Karen Duncan of Franklin, Nebraska. "We like it in summer when we don't want to heat up the house."

    1 pound ground beef
    1 celery rib, chopped
    1 medium onion, chopped
    ¼ cup chopped green pepper
    1 can (10½ ounces) pizza sauce
Salt to taste
    ¾ cup biscuit/baking mix
    3–4 tablespoons milk
    ¾ cup shredded mozzarella cheese
    2 tablespoons grated Parmesan cheese

Crumble beef into a microwave-safe 9-in. pie plate. Sprinkle with celery, onion and green pepper. Cover and microwave on high for 7 minutes or until meat is no longer pink and vegetables are tender, stirring once; drain. Stir in the pizza sauce and salt. Stir biscuit mix and milk just until combined. Roll out on a lightly floured surface into a 9-in. circle; place over meat mixture. Cook, uncovered, on high for 8 minutes or until a toothpick inserted into crust comes out clean. Invert onto a serving plate. Sprinkle with cheeses. **Yield:** 4 servings.

Sweet-and-Sour Meat Loaf

"I combined a few great-tasting meat loaf recipes to create this flavorful family favorite," says Deb Thompson of Lincoln, Nebraska. *"Because it's made in the microwave, it's ideal for busy nights."*

    1 egg
    5 tablespoons ketchup, *divided*
    2 tablespoons prepared mustard
    ½ cup dry bread crumbs
    2 tablespoons onion soup mix
    ¼ teaspoon salt
    ¼ teaspoon pepper
    1 pound ground beef
    ¼ cup sugar
    2 tablespoons brown sugar
    2 tablespoons cider vinegar

In a bowl, lightly beat the egg. Add 2 tablespoons of ketchup, mustard, bread crumbs, dry soup mix, salt and pepper. Crumble beef over mixture and mix well. Shape into an oval loaf. Place in a shallow 1-qt. microwave-safe dish; cover with waxed paper. Microwave on high for 11–12 minutes or until meat is no longer pink, rotating a half turn once; drain. In a small bowl, combine the sugars, vinegar and remaining ketchup; drizzle over meat loaf. Cover and microwave on high for 3–5 minutes. Let stand for 10 minutes before slicing. **Yield:** 4 servings.

Creamed Ham on Corn Bread

Denise Hershman of Cromwell, Indiana tops pieces of corn bread with a cheesy sauce chock-full of ham to make a satisfying and economical supper. "This is one budget meal our family loves," she writes.

    1 package (8½ ounces) corn bread/muffin mix
    1 egg
    ⅓ cup milk

CREAMED HAM:
    2 tablespoons butter
    2 tablespoons all-purpose flour
    ½ teaspoon ground mustard
    ¼ teaspoon salt
    1½ cups milk
    ¾ cup shredded cheddar cheese
    1½ cups cubed fully cooked ham

In a bowl, combine corn bread mix, egg and milk until blended. Spread into a greased 8-in. square baking pan. Bake at 400° for 18–20 minutes. Meanwhile, in a saucepan, melt butter; stir in flour, mustard and salt until smooth. Add milk. Bring to a boil; boil and stir for 2 minutes. Stir in cheese until melted. Add ham and heat through. Cut corn bread into squares; top with creamed ham. **Yield:** 6 servings.

Taco Noodle Dinner

Taco seasoning provides the family-appealing flavor in this speedy skillet supper shared by Marcy Cella of L'Anse, Michigan. The sour cream topping enhances this combination nicely.

1 pound ground beef
¼ cup chopped onion
¾ cup water
1 envelope taco seasoning
½ teaspoon salt
1 can (4 ounces) mushroom stems and pieces, drained
3 cups uncooked fine egg noodles
2½–3 cups tomato juice
1 cup (8 ounces) sour cream
1 tablespoon minced fresh parsley

In a large skillet over medium heat, cook the beef and onion until meat is no longer pink; drain. Stir in the water, taco seasoning and salt. Reduce heat; simmer for 2–3 minutes. Add the mushrooms. Sprinkle noodles over the top. Pour tomato juice over the noodles and stir gently. Cover and simmer for 20–25 minutes or until noodles are tender. Remove from the heat. Combine the sour cream and parsley; spread over the top. Cover and let stand for 5 minutes. **Yield:** 6 servings.

Cheesy Chicken Subs

"I've been part of the Food Services staff at Appalachian State University for 33 years," notes Jane Hollar of Vilas, North Carolina. "One summer we created this flavorful sandwich that combines seasoned grilled chicken, Swiss cheese and sauteed mushrooms and onions. Thousands of students have enjoyed this wonderful sub since then."

12 ounces boneless skinless chicken breasts, cut into strips
1 envelope Parmesan Italian *or* Caesar salad dressing mix
1 cup sliced fresh mushrooms
½ cup sliced red onion
¼ cup olive oil
4 submarine sandwich rolls, split and toasted
4 slices Swiss cheese

Place chicken in a bowl; sprinkle with salad dressing mix. In a skillet, saute mushrooms and onion in oil for 3 minutes. Add chicken; saute for 6 minutes or until chicken juices run clear. Spoon mixture onto roll bottoms; top with cheese. Broil 4 in. from heat for 4 minutes or until cheese is melted. Replace tops. **Yield:** 4 servings.

Chicken-Pesto Pan Pizza

A packaged pesto mix replaces traditional tomato sauce in this tempting pizza from Juanita Fleck. "Served with a tossed salad, this is one of my husband's favorite meals," says the Bullhead City, Arizona cook.

1 tube (10 ounces) **refrigerated pizza crust**
½ cup **water**
3 tablespoons **olive oil**
1 envelope **pesto sauce mix**
1 package (10 ounces) **frozen chopped spinach, thawed and squeezed dry**
½ cup **ricotta cheese**
¼ cup **chopped onion**
2 cups **shredded cooked chicken**
1 jar (4½ ounces) **sliced mushrooms, drained**
4 **plum tomatoes, sliced**
1 cup (4 ounces) **shredded Swiss cheese**
¼ cup **grated Romano cheese**

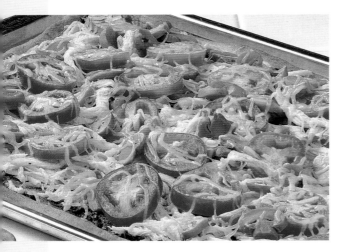

Unroll pizza crust into an ungreased 15-in. × 10-in. × 1-in. baking pan; flatten dough and build up edges slightly. Prick dough several times with a fork. Bake at 425° for 7 minutes or until lightly browned. Meanwhile, combine the water, oil and pesto sauce mix in a saucepan. Cook until heated through (do not boil). Add the spinach, ricotta and onion; mix well. Spread over crust. Top with chicken, mushrooms, tomatoes and Swiss and Romano cheeses. Bake at 425° for 7 minutes or until crust is golden and cheese is melted. **Yield:** 6–8 servings.

Sunday Chicken and Stuffing

This hearty entree from Charlotte Kidd of Lagrange, Ohio is a surefire family pleaser. "It's easy to prepare because you don't have to brown the chicken," she explains. "Plus it looks so nice you can serve it to company."

1 package (6 ounces) **instant chicken stuffing mix**
6 **boneless skinless chicken breast halves**
1 can (10¾ ounces) **condensed cream of chicken soup, undiluted**
⅓ cup **milk**
1 tablespoon **dried parsley flakes**

Prepare stuffing according to package directions; spoon down the center of a greased 13-in. × 9-in. × 2-in. baking dish. Place chicken around stuffing. Combine soup, milk and parsley; pour over chicken. Cover and bake at 400° for 20 minutes. Uncover and bake 10–15 minutes longer or until chicken juices run clear. **Yield:** 6 servings.

Italian Orange Roughy

"My family loves this moist and tender fish swimming in a flavorful sauce," says Alice Mashek of Schaumburg, Illinois. "It's easy to marinate first, then cook quickly in the microwave."

1 pound orange roughy fillets
½ cup tomato juice
2 tablespoons white vinegar
1 envelope Italian salad dressing mix
¼ cup chopped green onions
¼ cup chopped green pepper

Place fish fillets in a shallow 2-qt. microwave-safe dish, positioning the thickest portion of fish toward the outside edges. Combine tomato juice, vinegar and salad dressing mix; pour over fish. Cover and refrigerate for 30 minutes. Sprinkle with onions and green pepper. Cover and microwave on high for 3 minutes. Turn fillets over; cook 2–4 minutes longer or until fish flakes easily with a fork. Let stand, covered, for 2 minutes. **Yield:** 4 servings.

Pesto Chicken Penne

A convenient pesto sauce mix provides the pleasant basil flavor in this simple chicken and pasta combination from Beth Martin Sine of Faulkner, Maryland. This entree requires little effort, yet seems elegant.

8 ounces penne *or* any medium pasta
1 envelope pesto sauce mix
¾ cup milk
¼ cup olive oil
2 cups cubed cooked chicken *or* turkey
Shredded Parmesan cheese

Cook the pasta according to package directions. Meanwhile, in a large saucepan, whisk together pesto mix, milk and oil. Bring to a boil. Reduce heat; simmer, uncovered, for 5 minutes. Add chicken; heat through. Drain pasta. Add to the sauce and toss to coat. Sprinkle with cheese. **Yield:** 4–6 servings.

Santa Fe Enchiladas

"These flavorful enchiladas are my sister's favorite—she requests them whenever we get together," notes Lisa Zamora of Beloit, Wisconsin. *This meaty main dish is cooked in the microwave, so it's done in a jiffy.*

1½ pounds lean ground beef
1 medium onion, chopped
1 can (12 ounces) tomato paste
1 cup water
1 envelope taco seasoning
10 flour tortillas (6 inches), warmed
1 jar (8 ounces) process cheese sauce
1 can (4 ounces) chopped green chilies, drained

Crumble beef into a large microwave-safe bowl; stir in onion. Cover and microwave on high for 6–7½ minutes or until meat is no longer pink, stirring every 1½ minutes; drain. Stir in tomato paste, water and taco seasoning. Cover and cook on high for 3–4 minutes or until heated through, stirring once. Spoon about ⅓ cup meat mixture down the center of each tortilla; roll up tightly. Set remaining meat mixture aside. Place tortillas, seam side down, in a greased shallow 2½-qt. dish. In a microwave-safe bowl, combine cheese sauce and chilies. Cover and cook on high for 1 minute; stir. Pour over tortillas. Spoon remaining meat mixture down the center of tortillas. Cover and cook on high for 5–6 minutes or until heated through. Let stand 5 minutes before serving. **Yield:** 5 servings. **Editor's Note:** This recipe was tested in an 850-watt microwave.

Garlic Potatoes and Ham

"Not even my finicky little eaters can resist the veggies in this main dish when they're seasoned with soup mix," shares Melody Williamson of Blaine, Washington. *"I sometimes replace the ham with cooked kielbasa or smoked sausage for a change of pace."*

8 small red potatoes, cut into wedges
1 tablespoon vegetable oil
1 package (16 ounces) frozen broccoli cuts, partially thawed
1 cup cubed fully cooked ham
1 envelope herb with garlic soup mix

In a large skillet, cook potatoes in oil over medium-high heat for 10 minutes or until lightly browned. Stir in broccoli, ham and dry soup mix. Reduce heat; cover and cook for 25 minutes or until potatoes are tender. **Yield:** 4 servings. **Editor's Note:** This recipe was tested with Lipton Recipe Secrets Savory Herb with Garlic soup mix.

Pinto Bean Casserole

"With nine mouths to feed in my family, I'm always looking for speedy recipes," says Sherry Lee of Shelby, Alabama. *"This tasty casserole pleases everyone, from the kids to my husband."*

1 package (9 ounces) tortilla chips
2 cans (30 ounces *each*) pinto beans, rinsed and drained
1 can (15 ounces) whole kernel corn, drained
1 can (14½ ounces) diced tomatoes, drained
1 can (8 ounces) tomato sauce
1 envelope taco seasoning
2 cups (8 ounces) shredded cheddar cheese
Shredded lettuce, sour cream and salsa, optional

Crush tortilla chips and sprinkle into a greased 13-in. × 9-in. × 2-in. baking dish. In a large bowl, combine beans, corn, tomatoes, tomato sauce and taco seasoning; mix well. Pour over chips. Sprinkle with cheese. Bake, uncovered, at 350° for 18–25 minutes or until heated through. Serve with lettuce, sour cream and salsa if desired. **Yield:** 6–8 servings.

Cheesy Broccoli Pie

Biscuit mix is the secret to the no-fuss crust in this tasty broccoli dish shared by Judy Siegrist of Albuquerque, New Mexico. "There's no need to roll out a crust—it makes its own as it bakes," she says. "I keep one pie in the freezer to thaw and warm up in a jiffy."

2 packages (10 ounces *each*) frozen chopped broccoli, thawed
3 cups (12 ounces) shredded cheddar cheese, *divided*
⅔ cup chopped onion
3 eggs
1⅓ cups milk
¾ cup biscuit/baking mix
½ teaspoon salt
¼ teaspoon pepper

In a large bowl, combine broccoli, 2 cups cheese and onion. In another bowl, combine eggs, milk, biscuit mix, salt and pepper; mix well. Pour over broccoli mixture; toss gently. Pour into two greased 9-in. pie plates. Bake at 400° for 25–30 minutes or until a knife inserted near the center comes out clean. Sprinkle with remaining cheese; return to the oven for 1–2 minutes or until melted. Let stand 5–10 minutes before cutting. **Yield:** 2 pies (6 servings each).
Editor's Note: Baked pies may be frozen after cooling completely. To reheat, thaw and bake at 400° for 15–20 minutes or until heated through.

Cheesy Beef 'n' Noodles

Shredded cheese, diced tomatoes and whole kernel corn jazz up ground beef in this satisfying skillet supper from Nikki Detwiler of Lancaster, Ohio.

1 pound ground beef
4 cups uncooked wide egg noodles
1 can (28 ounces) diced tomatoes, undrained
½ cup water
¼ cup diced celery
¼ cup whole kernel corn
1 envelope onion soup mix
1 garlic clove, minced
1 cup (4 ounces) shredded process cheese (Velveeta)

In a large skillet, cook beef over medium heat until no longer pink; drain. Add noodles, tomatoes, water, celery, corn, dry soup mix and garlic. Bring to a boil. Reduce heat; cover and simmer for 20 minutes or until noodles are tender. Remove from the heat; sprinkle with cheese. Cover and let stand for 5 minutes or until cheese is melted. **Yield:** 4–6 servings.

Chili Nacho Supper

"The recipe for this creamy, chili-like dish was passed down through our church years ago," says Laurie Withers of Wildomar, California. *"It's so warm and filling that we often prepare it when we take skiing trips to Colorado."* It can be served over corn chips and eaten with a fork…or kept warm in a slow cooker and served as a hearty dip at parties.

2½ **pounds ground beef**
3 **cans (15 ounces *each*) tomato sauce**
2 **cans (16 ounces *each*) pinto beans, rinsed and drained**
1 **can (10 ounces) diced tomatoes and green chilies, undrained**
2 **envelopes chili mix**
2 **pounds process American cheese, cubed**
1 **cup heavy whipping cream**
2 **packages (16 ounces *each*) corn chips**
Sour cream

In a Dutch oven, cook the beef until no longer pink; drain. Add tomato sauce, beans, tomatoes and chili mix; heat through. Add cheese and cream; cook until the cheese is melted. Serve over chips. Top with sour cream. **Yield:** 14–16 servings.

Chicken and Rice

Crunched for time? Consider this fast-to-fix chicken-and-rice bake from Doris Barb of El Dorado, Kansas. After popping it in the oven, you can toss together a salad and have dinner on the table in no time.

6 **boneless skinless chicken breast halves**
1½ **cups uncooked instant rice**
½ **cup boiling water**
1 **can (10¾ ounces) condensed cream of chicken soup, undiluted**
1 **can (10¾ ounces) condensed cream of celery soup, undiluted**
2 **tablespoons onion soup mix**
1 **package (10 ounces) frozen peas, thawed**
½ **cup minced fresh parsley**

Place chicken in a greased 13-in. × 9-in. × 2-in. baking dish. In a bowl, combine rice and water. In another bowl, combine soups, dry soup mix and peas; stir into rice mixture. Spread over chicken. Cover and bake at 350° for 40 minutes. Uncover; sprinkle with parsley. Bake 10–15 minutes longer or until chicken juices run clear. **Yield:** 6 servings.

Taco Mac

Pork sausage, taco seasoning and taco sauce add plenty of zip to easy macaroni and cheese. "This zesty dish is just as yummy the next day," notes JoLynn Fribley of Oakley, Illinois. "Just warm it up and garnish with shredded lettuce, diced tomatoes and cheese."

  1 package (24 ounces) shells and cheese mix
½ pound bulk pork sausage, cooked and drained
⅓ cup taco sauce
  1 tablespoon taco seasoning
  4 cups shredded lettuce
  2 medium tomatoes, chopped
  1 cup (4 ounces) shredded cheddar cheese, optional

Prepare shells and cheese mix according to package directions. Stir in sausage, taco sauce and seasoning. Garnish with lettuce, tomatoes and cheddar cheese if desired. Serve immediately. **Yield:** 6 servings. **Editor's Note:** This recipe was tested with Kraft Velveeta Family-Size Shells & Cheese.

Lamb Ratatouille

"This quick-and-easy recipe is a great way to use up leftover lamb—and so good, your family will never guess it's a second-day dish," assures Maxine Cenker of Weirton, West Virginia. "It's also good with beef," she adds.

  1 package (6.9 ounces) beef-flavored rice mix
  2 tablespoons butter
2½ cups water
  3 medium tomatoes, peeled, seeded and chopped
  1 medium zucchini, sliced
1½ cups sliced fresh mushrooms
  1 small onion, chopped
  6 green onions, sliced
  3 garlic cloves, minced
  2 tablespoons olive oil
  1 pound cooked lamb *or* beef, cut into thin strips

Set rice seasoning packet aside. In a large skillet, saute the rice mix in butter until browned. Stir in water and contents of seasoning packet; bring to a boil. Reduce heat; cover and simmer for 15 minutes. Meanwhile, in another skillet, saute vegetables and garlic in oil until crisp-tender. Add lamb and vegetables to the rice. Cover and simmer for 5–10 minutes or until rice is tender. **Yield:** 4–6 servings.

Pork Sausage Puff

"I like to serve this special dish to overnight guests because I can prepare it the night before," notes Christina French of Elkhart, Indiana. *"The recipe, which I changed a bit to suit our family's tastes, came from a dear lady at our church."*

1 cup biscuit/baking mix
6 eggs, beaten
2 cups milk
2½ cups cooked bulk pork sausage (1 pound uncooked)
1 cup (4 ounces) shredded cheddar cheese
½ teaspoon dried oregano

In a bowl, combine the biscuit mix, eggs and milk until blended. Add the cooked sausage, cheese and oregano. Transfer to a greased 13-in. × 9-in. × 2-in. baking dish. Bake, uncovered, at 350° for 50–55 minutes or until a knife inserted near the center comes out clean. **Yield:** 6 servings. **Editor's Note:** This recipe can be prepared and refrigerated overnight. Remove from the refrigerator 30 minutes before baking.

Idaho Tacos

In Ozona, Texas, Kaleta Shepperson loads her potatoes with a taco topping that's quick, easy and flavorful. "Everyone who tries these potatoes likes them," she comments. "They're almost a meal by themselves. I serve them with breadsticks, a green salad and dessert."

1 pound ground beef
1 envelope taco seasoning
4 hot baked potatoes
1 cup (4 ounces) shredded sharp cheddar cheese
1 cup chopped green onions
Salsa, optional

In a skillet, brown beef; drain. Add taco seasoning; prepare according to package directions. With a sharp knife, cut an X in the top of each potato; fluff pulp with a fork. Top with taco meat, cheese and onions. Serve with salsa if desired. **Yield:** 4 servings.

Crustless Zucchini Pie

Peggy Gandy of South Amboy, New Jersey makes the most of her zucchini harvest by baking this crowd-pleasing entree. The golden-brown pies slice so beautifully you can serve them to company!

1 large onion, finely chopped
½ cup vegetable oil
½ cup grated Parmesan cheese
4 eggs, beaten
1 tablespoon minced fresh parsley
3 cups grated zucchini
1 cup biscuit/baking mix
1 cup (4 ounces) shredded cheddar cheese

In a bowl, combine the first five ingredients. Stir in the zucchini, biscuit mix and cheese. Pour into two greased 9-in. pie plates. Bake at 350° for 35 minutes or until golden brown. **Yield:** 2 pies (6 servings each).

Octopus and Seaweed

"I use ordinary hot dogs and fast-to-fix ramen noodles to create Octopus and Seaweed for my daughters," says Kerry Tittle of Little Rock, Arkansas. "Slice the hot dogs partway before cooking. When you drop them into boiling water, it will cause the strips to curl and create tentacles. A little green food coloring transforms the noodles into a bed of seaweed for the octopus to rest on. To add to the ocean theme, we serve this with fish shapes we've cut out of slices of American cheese."

1 package (3 ounces) beef ramen noodles
4 hot dogs
5 drops liquid green food coloring, optional
Prepared mustard

In a saucepan, bring 1½ cups water to a boil. Add the noodles and contents of seasoning packet. Boil for 3–4 minutes or until noodles are tender. Meanwhile, add 4 in. of water to a large saucepan; bring to a boil. Cut each hot dog lengthwise into eight strips to within 2 in. of one end. Drop into boiling water; cook until heated through. Add food coloring to noodles if desired. Drain if necessary. Place noodles on serving plates; top with a hot dog. Add eyes and mouth with dabs of mustard. **Yield:** 4 servings.

Chicken Noodle Stir-Fry

Darlene Markel of Sublimity, Oregon relies on Ramen noodles to stretch this appealing stir-fry. "You can use whatever vegetables you happen to have on hand," she suggests. "The dish is different every time I make it."

1 package (3 ounces) chicken-flavored Ramen noodles
1 pound boneless skinless chicken breasts, cut into strips
1 tablespoon vegetable oil
1 cup broccoli florets
1 cup cauliflowerets
1 cup sliced celery
1 cup coarsely chopped cabbage
2 medium carrots, thinly sliced
1 medium onion, thinly sliced
½ cup fresh *or* canned bean sprouts
½ cup teriyaki *or* soy sauce

Set aside seasoning packet from noodles. Cook noodles according to package directions. Meanwhile, in a large skillet or wok, stir-fry chicken in oil for 5–6 minutes or until no longer pink. Add vegetables; stir-fry for 3–4 minutes or until crisp-tender. Drain noodles; add to the pan with contents of seasoning packet and the teriyaki sauce. Stir well. Serve immediately. **Yield:** 4 servings.

MAIN DISHES

French Dip Sandwiches

When Florence Robinson of Lenox, Iowa wants to impress company, she puts these sandwiches on the menu. "I serve the au jus sauce in individual bowls for dipping. It's delicious," she assures.

2 large onions, cut into ¼-inch slices
¼ cup butter
1 boneless bottom round roast (3 to 4 pounds)
5 cups water
½ cup soy sauce
1 envelope onion soup mix
1½ teaspoons browning sauce, optional
1 garlic clove, minced
12–14 French rolls, split
1 cup (4 ounces) shredded Swiss cheese

In a skillet, saute onions in butter until tender; transfer to a slow cooker. Cut the roast in half; place over onions. Combine water, soy sauce, dry soup mix, browning sauce if desired and garlic; pour over roast. Cover and cook on low for 7–9 hours or until the meat is tender. Remove roast with a slotted spoon and let stand for 15 minutes. Thinly slice meat across the grain. Place on rolls; sprinkle with Swiss cheese. Broil 3 to 4 in. from the heat for 1 minute or until the cheese is melted. Skim fat from the cooking juices; strain and serve as a dipping sauce. **Yield:** 12–14 servings.

Sausage Potatoes Au Gratin

A packaged potato mix gets special treatment when jazzed up with sausage and vegetables. "I enjoy serving this cheesy casserole with warm bread," informs Mary Akker of Ellsworth, Minnesota.

1 pound fully cooked smoked sausage, halved
　lengthwise and sliced
1 medium onion, chopped
1 tablespoon vegetable oil
4 medium carrots, julienned
1 package (5¼ ounces) au gratin potatoes
2⅔ cups water
¼ teaspoon pepper
1 package (10 ounces) frozen broccoli cuts, thawed
　and drained
1 cup (4 ounces) shredded cheddar cheese

In a large saucepan or Dutch oven, cook sausage and onion in oil until lightly browned; drain. Stir in carrots, potatoes with contents of sauce mix, water and pepper. Bring to a boil. Reduce heat; cover and simmer for 10–20 minutes or until vegetables are tender. Stir in broccoli; cover and cook 5 minutes longer or until heated through. Sprinkle with cheese; cover and let stand until cheese is melted. **Yield:** 4 servings.

Chicken Fried Rice

In Maplecrest, New York, Kathy Hoyt relies on a fried rice mix to start this speedy skillet supper. It makes the most of leftover cooked chicken and a can of crunchy water chestnuts.

1 package (6.2 ounces) fried rice mix
2 cups cubed cooked chicken
1½ cups cooked broccoli florets
1 can (8 ounces) sliced water chestnuts, drained
1 cup (4 ounces) shredded mozzarella cheese

Cook rice according to package directions. Stir in chicken, broccoli and water chestnuts; heat through. Sprinkle with cheese. **Yield:** 4 servings.

Ham Macaroni Salad

"I made some changes to the original recipe by adding extra tomatoes for more color, celery for crunch, relish for a hint of sweetness and ham to make it more filling," explains Karen Ballance of Wolf Lake, Illinois. "It's great for picnics and potlucks or as a side dish for any meal," she adds. "It's also handy because you make it ahead of time."

1 package (7½ ounces) macaroni and cheese
½ cup mayonnaise
2 tablespoons Dijon mustard
3 medium tomatoes, seeded and chopped
1 medium cucumber, peeled and chopped
1 cup diced fully cooked ham
4 hard-cooked eggs, chopped
½ cup chopped celery
¼ cup sweet pickle relish
2 tablespoons chopped onion
½ teaspoon salt
⅛ teaspoon pepper

Prepare macaroni and cheese according to package directions; cool for 20 minutes. Stir in the mayonnaise and mustard. Fold in the remaining ingredients. Refrigerate for 2 hours or until chilled. **Yield:** 8 servings.

Shrimp Curry Rice

"There aren't any left-overs when I serve my family this fast and easy dish," says Sandi Rush of Athens, Texas. Convenient canned or frozen shrimp rounds out the flavors of this quick but classic entree.

2⅓ cups water
1 tablespoon butter
1 package (6 ounces) long grain and wild rice mix
½ teaspoon curry powder
1 can (6 ounces) small shrimp, rinsed and drained
   or 1 cup frozen cooked salad shrimp
4 bacon strips, cooked and crumbled

Place water and butter in a large saucepan; stir in rice, contents of rice seasoning packet and curry powder. Bring to a boil. Reduce heat; cover and simmer for 15 minutes. Add shrimp and bacon. Cover and simmer 10 minutes longer or until liquid is absorbed and rice is tender. **Yield:** 2–3 servings.

Spicy Shepherd's Pie

"To save time, I cook the beef, vegetables and onion together, then freeze it to use later," says Paula Zsiray of Logan, Utah. "On a hectic day, I pull the meat mixture for this family-pleasing pie out of the freezer to thaw."

1 package (6.6 ounces) instant mashed potatoes
1 pound ground beef
1 medium onion, chopped
1 can (14½ ounces) diced tomatoes, undrained
1 can (11 ounces) Mexicorn, drained
1 can (2¼ ounces) sliced ripe olives, drained
1 envelope taco seasoning
1½ teaspoons chili powder
½ teaspoon salt
⅛ teaspoon garlic powder
1 cup (4 ounces) shredded cheddar cheese, *divided*

Prepare mashed potatoes according to package directions. Meanwhile, in a large skillet, cook beef and onion until the meat is browned; drain. Add tomatoes, corn, olives, taco seasoning, chili powder, salt and garlic powder. Bring to a boil; cook and stir for 1–2 minutes. Transfer to a greased 2½-qt. baking dish. Top with ¾ cup cheese. Spread mashed potatoes over the top; sprinkle with remaining cheese. Bake, uncovered, at 350° for 12–15 minutes or until cheese is melted. **Yield:** 4–6 servings. **Editor's Note:** 4½ cups hot mashed potatoes (prepared with milk and butter) may be substituted for the instant mashed potatoes.

Giant Stuffed Picnic Burger

Guests will be delighted when they sink their teeth into juicy wedges of this full-flavored burger shared by Helen Hudson of Brockville, Ontario. The moist filling is chock-full of mushrooms, onion and parsley. "It's a great alternative to regular burgers," she remarks.

2 pounds ground beef
1 teaspoon salt
1 teaspoon Worcestershire sauce
¾ cup crushed seasoned stuffing mix
1 can (4 ounces) mushroom stems and pieces, drained
¼ cup beef broth
¼ cup minced fresh parsley
¼ cup sliced green onions
1 egg, beaten
1 tablespoon butter, melted
1 teaspoon lemon juice

Combine beef, salt and Worcestershire sauce. Divide in half; pat each half into an 8-in. circle on waxed paper. Combine the remaining ingredients; spoon over one patty to within 1 in. of the edge. Top with second patty; press edges to seal. Grill, covered, over medium heat for 12–13 minutes on each side or until the juices run clear. Cut into wedges. **Yield:** 6 servings.

Editor's Note: Stuffed burger may be placed directly on the grill or in a well-greased wire grill basket.

Wild Rice Mushroom Chicken

Jacqueline Thompson Graves of Lawrenceville, Georgia uses a wild rice mix to put a tasty spin on a traditional chicken-and-rice bake. "It's simple and delicious," she says. "It's also yummy made with leftover chicken or turkey."

2 packages (6 ounces *each*) long grain and wild rice mix
8 boneless skinless chicken breast halves
5 tablespoons butter, *divided*
1 large sweet red pepper, chopped
2 jars (4½ ounces *each*) sliced mushrooms, drained

Prepare rice according to package directions. Meanwhile, in a large skillet, cook chicken in 3 tablespoons butter for 10 minutes on each side or until browned and juices run clear. Remove chicken and keep warm. Add remaining butter to pan drippings; saute red pepper until tender. Stir in mushrooms; heat through. Add to rice. Serve four chicken breasts with half of the rice mixture. Place remaining chicken in a greased 11-in. × 7-in. × 2-in. baking dish; top with remaining rice mixture. Cool. Cover and freeze for up to 3 months. **To use frozen dish:** Thaw in the refrigerator. Cover and bake at 350° for 35–40 minutes or until heated through. **Yield:** 2 dishes (4 servings each).

MAIN DISHES

Herbed Pork and Potatoes

From Charlestown, Massachusetts, Evelyn Harzbecker sends this hearty combination of pork, stuffing and vegetables. "With red tomatoes and green parsley, it's a colorful meal in one," says Evelyn.

½ cup butter, *divided*
3 cups cubed red potatoes (1-inch pieces)
1 pound boneless pork loin, cut into 1-inch cubes
½ teaspoon dried rosemary, crushed
½ teaspoon rubbed sage
½ teaspoon salt
½ teaspoon pepper
1 garlic clove, minced
2 cups crushed herb-seasoned stuffing
1 cup sliced celery
1 cup chopped onion
½ cup apple juice
3 medium tomatoes, chopped
¼ cup minced fresh parsley

In a large skillet, melt ¼ cup butter. Add potatoes; cook over medium heat, stirring occasionally, until lightly browned. Add pork, rosemary, sage, salt, pepper and garlic. Cook and stir until pork is browned, about 12 minutes. Add stuffing, celery, onion, apple juice and remaining butter; stir well. Cover and cook for 7 minutes or until heated through. Stir in tomatoes and parsley. Remove from the heat; cover and let stand for 2 minutes. **Yield:** 4 servings.

Turkey Stuffing Roll-Ups

"When I worked at a local deli, a customer gave me this family-pleasing recipe," recalls Darlene Ward of Hot Springs, Arkansas. "After a busy day, I tried it with quicker boxed stuffing mix in place of homemade dressing. It's wonderful with salad and green beans."

1 package (6 ounces) stuffing mix
1 can (10¾ ounces) condensed cream of chicken soup, undiluted
¾ cup milk
1 pound sliced deli smoked turkey
1 can (2.8 ounces) french-fried onions, crushed

Prepare stuffing mix according to package directions. Meanwhile, in a bowl, combine soup and milk; set aside. Spoon about ¼ cup stuffing onto each turkey slice. Roll up and place in a greased 13-in. × 9-in. × 2-in. baking dish. Pour soup mixture over roll-ups. Bake, uncovered, at 350° for 20 minutes. Sprinkle with onions. Bake 5 minutes longer or until heated through. **Yield:** 6 servings. **Editor's Note:** 3 cups of any prepared stuffing can be substituted for the stuffing mix.

Herbed Chicken Fettuccine

Savory seasonings add zip to these moist chicken strips tossed with pasta. "Every time I fix this dish, the kids ask for more," reports Kathy Kirkland of Denham Springs, Louisiana. "It goes well with steamed broccoli and glazed carrots to make a quick and colorful meal."

1–2 teaspoons salt-free seasoning blend
  1 teaspoon poultry seasoning
  1 pound boneless skinless chicken breasts, cut into 1-inch strips
  2 tablespoons olive oil
  4 tablespoons butter, *divided*
 ⅔ cup water
  2 tablespoons teriyaki sauce
  2 tablespoons onion soup mix
  1 envelope savory herb and garlic soup mix, *divided*
  8 ounces uncooked fettuccine *or* pasta of your choice
  2 tablespoons grated Parmesan cheese
  1 tablespoon Worcestershire sauce

Combine seasoning blend and poultry seasoning; sprinkle over chicken. In a skillet, saute chicken in oil and 2 tablespoons butter for 5 minutes or until juices run clear. Add the water, teriyaki sauce, onion soup mix and 2 tablespoons herb and garlic soup mix. Bring to a boil. Reduce heat; cover and simmer for 15 minutes. Meanwhile, cook the fettuccine according to package directions. Drain; add to the chicken mixture. Add cheese, Worcestershire sauce, remaining butter, and remaining herb and garlic soup mix; toss to coat. **Yield:** 4 servings.

Chicken 'n' Biscuits

"This cheesy chicken casserole gets its vibrant color from frozen vegetables and its unique flavor from crumbled bacon," reports Debbie Vannette of Zeeland, Michigan. "The biscuit-topped dish has become a regular at our dinner table since my sister-in-law shared it with us after the birth of our son."

1 package (16 ounces) frozen mixed vegetables
2½ cups cubed cooked chicken
1 can (10¾ ounces) condensed cream of chicken soup, undiluted
¾ cup milk
1½ cups (6 ounces) shredded cheddar cheese, *divided*
8 bacon strips, cooked and crumbled, optional

BISCUITS:
1½ cups biscuit/baking mix
⅔ cup milk
1 can (2.8 ounces) french-fried onions

In a large bowl, combine the vegetables, chicken, soup, milk, 1 cup cheese and bacon if desired. Pour into an ungreased 13-in. × 9-in. × 2-in. baking dish. Cover and bake at 400° for 15 minutes. Meanwhile, in another bowl, combine biscuit mix and milk. Drop batter by tablespoonfuls onto chicken mixture. Bake, uncovered, for 20–22 minutes or until biscuits are golden brown. Top with onions and remaining cheese. Bake 3–4 minutes longer or until the cheese is melted. **Yield:** 6 servings.

Taco Meat Loaf

"Even your kids will enjoy this tasty meat loaf," promises Cathy Streeter of De Kalb Junction, New York. *"I like to serve it with shredded cheese, salsa and sour cream."*

1 cup crushed saltines (about 30 crackers)
1 envelope taco seasoning mix
½ cup ketchup
1 can (4 ounces) mushroom stems and pieces, drained
1 can (2¼ ounces) sliced ripe olives, drained
1 small onion, chopped
2 eggs, beaten
2 tablespoons Worcestershire sauce
2 pounds lean ground beef
Salsa, sour cream, shredded cheddar cheese and additional olives, optional

In a bowl, combine the first eight ingredients. Add beef; mix well. Press into a greased 9-in. × 5-in. × 3-in. loaf pan. Bake, uncovered, at 350° for 1 to 1½ hours or until a meat thermometer reads 160°. Serve with salsa, sour cream, cheese and olives if desired. **Yield:** 8 servings.

Salmon Macaroni Bake

"A neighbor brought us this creamy casserole the night after our new-born daughter came home from the hospital," recalls Carrie Mitchell of Raleigh, North Carolina. *"It was so good, we couldn't resist heating up the leftovers the next morning."*

1 package (14 ounces) deluxe macaroni and cheese dinner mix
1 can (10¾ ounces) condensed cream of mushroom soup, undiluted
½ cup milk
1 can (6 ounces) skinless boneless salmon, drained
1 tablespoon grated onion *or* ½ teaspoon onion powder
½ cup shredded cheddar cheese
½ cup dry bread crumbs
2 tablespoons butter, cubed

Prepare macaroni and cheese according to package directions. Stir in the soup, milk, salmon, onion and cheddar cheese. Transfer to a greased 1½-qt. baking dish. Sprinkle with bread crumbs; dot with butter. Bake, uncovered, at 375° for 30 minutes or until heated through. **Yield:** 4 servings.

Stuffed Flank Steak

Diane Hixon's elegant slow-cooked meal is worthy of company. "I like to make it on special occasions," she writes from Niceville, Florida. "The tender steak cuts easily into appetizing spirals for serving, and extra stuffing cooks conveniently in a foil packet on top of the steak."

1 package (8 ounces) crushed corn bread stuffing
1 cup chopped onion
1 cup chopped celery
¼ cup minced fresh parsley
2 eggs
1¼ cups beef broth
⅓ cup butter, melted
½ teaspoon seasoned salt
½ teaspoon pepper
1½ pounds flank steak

In a large bowl, combine stuffing, onion, celery and parsley. In a small bowl, beat the eggs; stir in broth and butter. Pour over stuffing mixture. Sprinkle with seasoned salt and pepper; stir well. Pound steak to ½-in. thickness. Spread 1½ cups stuffing mixture over steak. Roll up, starting with a short side; tie with string. Place in a 5-qt. slow cooker. Remaining stuffing can be wrapped tightly in foil and placed over the rolled steak. Cover and cook on low for 6–8 hours or until a meat thermometer inserted in stuffing reads 165°. Remove string before slicing. **Yield:** 6 servings. **Editor's Note:** No liquid is added to the slow cooker. The moisture comes from the meat.

Oregano Chicken

Salad dressing mix and a generous sprinkling of oregano add the rich herb flavor to this tender baked chicken from Nancy Moore of Candler, North Carolina. It's easy to prepare and great over rice or noodles.

¼ cup butter, melted
1 envelope Italian salad dressing mix
2 tablespoons lemon juice
1 broiler/fryer chicken (3½ to 4 pounds), cut up
1–2 tablespoons dried oregano

Combine the butter, salad dressing mix and lemon juice. Place chicken in an ungreased 13-in. × 9-in. × 2-in. baking dish. Spoon butter mixture over chicken. Cover and bake at 350° for 45 minutes. Uncover. Baste with pan drippings; sprinkle with oregano. Bake 15–20 minutes longer or until the chicken juices run clear. **Yield:** 6 servings.

Creamy Italian Chicken

From Tallahassee, Florida, Maura McGee shares her recipe for tender chicken in a creamy sauce that gets fast flavor from salad dressing mix. Served over rice or pasta, it's rich, delicious and special enough for company.

4 boneless skinless chicken breast halves
1 envelope Italian salad dressing mix
¼ cup water
1 package (8 ounces) cream cheese, softened
1 can (10¾ ounces) condensed cream of chicken soup, undiluted
1 can (4 ounces) mushroom stems and pieces, drained
Hot cooked rice *or* noodles

Place the chicken in a slow cooker. Combine salad dressing mix and water; pour over chicken. Cover and cook on low for 3 hours. In a small mixing bowl, beat cream cheese and soup until blended. Stir in mushrooms. Pour over chicken. Cook 1 hour longer or until chicken juices run clear. Serve over rice or noodles. **Yield:** 4 servings.

Quicker Pork Chops Over Stuffing

Here's a hearty dish with old-fashioned flavor but new-fashioned ingredients. The Taste of Home Test Kitchen used instant stuffing mix and boneless pork chops to make this comforting classic speedy and tasty!

2 packages (6 ounces *each*) instant stuffing mix
3⅓ cups chicken broth
½ cup butter
8 boneless pork loin chops (½ to ¾ inch thick)
Worcestershire sauce, optional
Minced fresh parsley, optional

In a large saucepan, combine the vegetable/seasoning packets from stuffing mix with broth and butter. Bring to a boil. Reduce heat; cover and simmer for 5 minutes. Stir in stuffing. Cover and remove from the heat; let stand for 5 minutes. Spoon stuffing into eight mounds in a greased 13-in. × 9-in. × 2-in. baking dish. Place a pork chop over each mound. Sprinkle with Worcestershire sauce if desired. Cover and bake at 425° for 15 minutes. Uncover; bake 20 minutes longer or until meat juices run clear. Garnish with parsley if desired. **Yield:** 8 servings.

Vegetarian Lasagna Loaf

"*I enjoy preparing this meatless casserole for my family,*" *relates Francine Scott of DeLand, Florida. "They love its creamy texture and think they're eating an extremely rich dish when in fact it's good for them.*"

5 no-cook lasagna noodles
2 envelopes (1¼ ounces *each*) white sauce mix
1 tablespoon Italian seasoning
1 teaspoon garlic powder
3 cups fat-free milk
1 cup (8 ounces) fat-free ricotta cheese
1 cup frozen California-blend vegetables, thawed
½ cup fat-free Parmesan cheese topping
2 tablespoons reduced-fat sour cream
½ cup seeded chopped fresh tomato

Break the noodles in half widthwise; set aside. In a saucepan, combine sauce mix, Italian seasoning and garlic powder. Gradually stir in milk. Bring to a boil; cook and stir for 2 minutes or until thickened and bubbly. In an 8-in. × 4-in. × 2-in. loaf pan coated with nonstick cooking spray, layer ½ cup sauce, two noodle pieces, ¼ cup ricotta cheese, ¼ cup vegetables and about 1½ tablespoons Parmesan cheese topping. Repeat layers three times. Top with remaining noodles, sour cream, ½ cup sauce, tomato and remaining Parmesan cheese topping. Bake, uncovered, at 350° for 30–35 minutes or until bubbly and noodles are tender. Let stand 10 minutes before serving. Reheat remaining sauce; serve with lasagna. **Yield:** 4 servings.

Savory Chicken Sandwiches

With eight young children, Joan Parker of Gastonia, North Carolina knows how to make family-pleasing meals. "This tender chicken tastes like you fussed, but requires few ingredients," she notes. You can also thicken the juices and serve it over rice.

4 bone-in chicken breast halves
4 chicken thighs
1 envelope onion soup mix
¼ teaspoon garlic salt
¼ cup prepared Italian salad dressing
¼ cup water
14–16 hamburger buns, split

Remove skin from chicken if desired. Place chicken in a 5-qt. slow cooker. Sprinkle with dry soup mix and garlic salt. Pour dressing and water over chicken. Cover and cook on low for 8–9 hours. Remove chicken; cool slightly. Skim fat from cooking juices. Remove chicken from bones; cut into bite-size pieces and return to slow cooker. Heat through. Use a slotted spoon to serve on buns. **Yield:** 14–16 servings.

Pepper Beef Goulash

Peggy Key of Grant, Alabama uses only a couple of common ingredients to turn beef stew meat into a hearty entree. No one will ever guess the secret behind her great goulash—an envelope of sloppy joe seasoning.

½ cup water
1 can (6 ounces) tomato paste
2 tablespoons cider vinegar
1 envelope sloppy joe seasoning
2–2¼ pounds beef stew meat (¾-inch cubes)
1 celery rib, cut into ½-inch slices
1 medium green pepper, cut into ½-inch chunks
Hot cooked noodles

In a slow cooker, combine the water, tomato paste, vinegar and sloppy joe seasoning. Stir in the beef, celery and green pepper. Cover and cook on high for 4–5 hours. Serve over noodles. Yield: 4–5 servings.

Cheesy Potato Beef Bake

"I created this layered meat-and-potatoes casserole a few years ago when my mother asked me what I wanted for supper," shares Nicole Rute. "My family thinks it tastes great," adds the Fall River, Wisconsin cook.

1 pound ground beef
2 cans (4 ounces *each*) mushroom stems and pieces, drained, optional
2 packages (5¼ ounces *each*) au gratin potatoes
4 cups boiling water
1⅓ cups milk
2 teaspoons butter
1 teaspoon salt
½ teaspoon seasoned salt
½ teaspoon pepper
1 cup (4 ounces) shredded cheddar cheese

In a skillet over medium heat, cook beef until no longer pink; drain. Place in a greased 13-in. × 9-in. × 2-in. baking pan. Top with mushrooms. Combine potatoes and contents of sauce mix packets, water, milk, butter, salt, seasoned salt and pepper. Pour over beef and mushrooms. Cover and bake at 400° for 30 minutes or until heated through. Sprinkle with cheese. Bake, uncovered, for 5 minutes or until cheese is melted. Let stand 10 minutes before serving. **Yield:** 8 servings.

Ham 'n' Cheese Pie

Mary Anderson, a 4-H leader from De Valls Bluff, Arkansas, shares family-pleasing fare that one of her 4-H students entered in a local contest. The recipe makes two easy-to-assemble pies that are tasty whether served morning, noon or night.

2 cups cubed fully cooked ham
2 cups (8 ounces) shredded cheddar cheese
1 cup chopped onion
4 eggs
2 cups milk
1 cup biscuit/baking mix
Dash pepper

Sprinkle ham, cheese and onion into two greased 9-in. pie plates. In a bowl, combine eggs, milk, biscuit mix and pepper until blended; pour over ham mixture. Bake at 400° for 35–40 minutes or until a knife inserted near the center comes out clean. Let stand for 5 minutes before cutting. **Yield:** 2 pies (4–6 servings each).

Roast Beef with Gravy

"Start this simple roast in the morning, and you'll have savory slices of meat and gravy ready at suppertime," notes Tracy Ashbeck of Wisconsin Rapids, Wisconsin. The tender beef is loaded with homemade taste and leaves plenty for main dishes later in the week.

1 boneless beef sirloin tip roast (about 4 pounds)
½ cup all-purpose flour, *divided*
1 envelope onion soup mix
1 envelope brown gravy mix
2 cups cold water
Hot mashed potatoes

Cut roast in half; rub with ¼ cup flour. Place in a 5-qt. slow cooker. In a bowl, combine soup and gravy mixes and remaining flour; stir in water until blended. Pour over roast. Cover and cook on low for 6–8 hours or until meat is tender. Slice roast; serve with mashed potatoes and gravy. **Yield:** 16 servings.

CHAPTER 5

Soups

Nacho Potato Soup

"This soup is super easy to make! Since it starts with a box of au gratin potatoes, you don't have to peel or slice them," notes *Sherry Dickerson of Sebastopol, Mississippi. "A co-worker shared this recipe with me."*

1 package (5¼ ounces) au gratin potatoes
1 can (11 ounces) whole kernel corn, drained
1 can (10 ounces) diced tomatoes and green chilies, undrained
2 cups water
2 cups milk
2 cups cubed process American cheese
Dash hot pepper sauce, optional
Minced fresh parsley, optional

In a 3-qt. saucepan, combine the potatoes and sauce mix, corn, tomatoes and water; mix well. Bring to a boil. Reduce heat; cover and simmer for 15–18 minutes or until potatoes are tender. Add milk, cheese and hot pepper sauce if desired; cook and stir until the cheese is melted. Garnish with parsley if desired. **Yield:** 6–8 servings (2 quarts).

Wild Rice Soup

"I tasted this thick and hearty soup at a food fair I helped judge," says *Kathy Herink of Gladbrook, Iowa. "It didn't earn a ribbon, but I thought it was a real winner. The original recipe called for uncooked wild rice, but instead I use a quick-cooking rice blend."*

1 pound ground beef
2 cups chopped celery
2 cups chopped onion
3 cups water
1 can (14½ ounces) chicken broth
1 can (10¾ ounces) condensed cream of mushroom soup, undiluted
1 package (6.75 ounces) quick-cooking long grain and wild rice mix
5 bacon strips, cooked and crumbled

In a 3-qt. saucepan, cook beef, celery and onion until beef is browned and vegetables are tender; drain. Add water, broth, soup and rice with contents of the seasoning packet. Bring to a boil. Reduce heat; cover and simmer for 5 minutes. Garnish with bacon. **Yield:** 8 servings (about 2 quarts).

Vegetable Beef Soup

This quick and colorful soup goes together in minutes, assures Agnes Bierbaum, Gainesville, Florida. "Even my husband—who admits he's no cook—makes it on occasion," she says.

½ **pound ground beef**
2 **cups water**
1 **can (14½ ounces) stewed tomatoes**
1 **package (10 ounces) frozen mixed vegetables**
1 **can (8 ounces) tomato sauce**
1 **envelope onion soup mix**
½ **teaspoon sugar**

In a saucepan over medium heat, cook beef until no longer pink; drain. Add the remaining ingredients; bring to a boil. Reduce heat; cover and simmer for 10–15 minutes or until the vegetables are tender. **Yield:** 6 servings.

Simple Taco Soup

"We first sampled this chili-like soup at a church dinner," informs Glenda Taylor of Sand Springs, Oklahoma. "It's a warming dish on a cold day, and since it uses packaged seasonings and several cans of vegetables, it's a snap to prepare."

2 **pounds ground beef**
1 **envelope taco seasoning mix**
1½ **cups water**
1 **can (15¾ ounces) mild chili beans**
1 **can (15¼ ounces) whole kernel corn, drained**
1 **can (15 ounces) pinto beans, rinsed and drained**
1 **can (14½ ounces) stewed tomatoes**
1 **can (10 ounces) diced tomatoes with green chilies**
1 **can (4 ounces) chopped green chilies, optional**
1 **envelope ranch salad dressing mix**

In a Dutch oven or large kettle, brown beef; drain. Add taco seasoning and mix well. Stir in remaining ingredients. Simmer, uncovered, for 15 minutes or until heated through, stirring occasionally. **Yield:** 6–8 servings (about 2 quarts).

Zesty Macaroni Soup

"The recipe for this thick, zippy soup first caught my attention for two reasons—it calls for ingredients that are found in my pantry, and it can be prepared in a jiffy, says Joan Hallford of North Richland Hills, Texas. "A chili macaroni mix provides this dish with a little spice, but sometimes I jazz it up with a can of chopped green chilies. It's a family favorite."

1 pound ground beef
1 medium onion, chopped
5 cups water
1 can (15 ounces) pinto beans, rinsed and drained
1 can (14½ ounces) diced tomatoes, undrained
1 can (7 ounces) whole kernel corn, drained
1 can (4 ounces) chopped green chilies, optional
½ teaspoon ground mustard
½ teaspoon salt
⅛ teaspoon pepper
1 package (7½ ounces) chili macaroni dinner mix
Salsa con queso dip

In a saucepan, cook beef and onion until meat is no longer pink; drain. Stir in water, beans, tomatoes, corn and chilies if desired. Stir in mustard, salt, pepper and contents of macaroni sauce mix. Bring to a boil. Reduce heat; cover and simmer for 10 minutes. Stir in contents of macaroni packet. Cover and simmer 10–14 minutes longer or until macaroni is tender, stirring once. Serve with salsa con queso dip. **Yield:** 8–10 servings (about 2½ quarts). **Editor's Note:** This recipe was tested with Hamburger Helper brand chili macaroni. Salsa con queso dip can be found in the international food section or snack aisle of most grocery stores.

Lasagna Soup

"This recipe is excellent for working mothers because it's fast to make and very flavorful," notes Gladys Shaffer of Elma, Washington. *Fresh zucchini and corn add color and crunch to a boxed lasagna dinner mix.*

1 pound ground beef
½ cup chopped onion
1 package (7¾ ounces) lasagna dinner mix
5 cups water
1 can (14½ ounces) diced tomatoes, undrained
1 can (7 ounces) whole kernel corn, undrained
2 tablespoons grated Parmesan cheese
1 small zucchini, chopped

In a Dutch oven or soup kettle, cook beef and onion over medium heat until meat is no longer pink; drain. Add contents of lasagna dinner sauce mix, water, tomatoes, corn and Parmesan cheese; bring to a boil. Reduce heat; cover and simmer for 10 minutes, stirring occasionally. Add the lasagna noodles and zucchini. Cover and simmer for 10 minutes or until noodles are tender. Serve immediately. **Yield:** 10 servings (2½ quarts).

Ground Beef Noodle Soup

This savory specialty combines ground beef with onions, celery and carrots. "This is a wonderful, fast soup to make any day of the week," says Judy Brander of Two Harbors, Minnesota.

1½ pounds ground beef
½ cup *each* chopped onion, celery and carrot
7 cups water
1 envelope au jus mix
2 tablespoons beef bouillon granules
2 bay leaves
⅛ teaspoon pepper
1½ cups uncooked egg noodles

In a large saucepan or Dutch oven, cook beef, onion, celery and carrot over medium heat until meat is no longer pink and vegetables are tender; drain. Add water, au jus mix, bouillon, bay leaves and pepper; bring to a boil. Stir in the noodles. Boil, uncovered, for 15 minutes or until noodles are tender, stirring occasionally. Discard bay leaves before serving. **Yield:** 8 servings (2 quarts).

Cheesy Wild Rice Soup

"We often eat easy-to-make soups when there's not a lot of time to cook," relates Lisa Hofer of Hitchcock, South Dakota. *"I replaced the wild rice requested in the original recipe with a boxed rice mix. This creamy concoction is now a family favorite."*

> 1 package (6 ounces) quick-cooking long grain and wild rice mix
> 4 cups milk
> 1 can (10¾ ounces) condensed cream of potato soup, undiluted
> 8 ounces process American cheese, cubed
> ½ pound sliced bacon, cooked and crumbled

In a large saucepan, prepare rice according to package directions. Stir in milk, soup and cheese; mix well. Cook and stir until cheese is melted. Garnish with bacon. **Yield:** 6–8 servings.

Chicken Dumpling Soup

"Although we were on a tight budget when I was a youngster, we always had good food," recalls Brenda Risser of Willard, Ohio. *"This comforting soup with soft dumplings was one of Mom's mainstays."*

> 2 cans (10¾ ounces *each*) condensed cream of chicken soup, undiluted
> 3⅓ cups milk, *divided*
> 1⅔ cups biscuit/baking mix

In a 3-qt. saucepan, combine soup and 2⅔ cups of milk. Bring to a boil over medium heat; reduce heat. In a bowl, combine biscuit mix with remaining milk just until blended. Drop by rounded tablespoons onto simmering soup. Cook, uncovered, for 10 minutes. Cover and simmer 10–12 minutes longer or until dumplings test done (do not lift lid while simmering). Serve immediately. **Yield:** 4 servings.

Tasty Turkey Soup

2 tablespoons chopped celery
2 tablespoons chopped onion
1 tablespoon butter
1 package (3 ounces) chicken-flavored ramen noodles
1½ cups water
1 can (10¾ ounces) condensed turkey noodle soup, undiluted
1 cup chicken broth
½ cup cubed cooked turkey
Pepper to taste

In a saucepan, saute celery and onion in butter until tender. Discard seasoning packet from ramen noodles or save for another use. Stir noodles, water, soup, broth, turkey and pepper into celery mixture. Cook for 3 minutes or until noodles are tender and heated through. **Yield:** 4 servings.

Beef Noodle Soup

In Lincoln, Nebraska, Arlene Lynn takes advantage of convenience items to prepare this hearty soup in a hurry. Bowls of the chunky mixture are chock-full of ground beef, noodles and vegetables.

1 pound ground beef
1 can (46 ounces) V8 juice
1 envelope onion soup mix
1 package (3 ounces) beef ramen noodles
1 package (16 ounces) frozen mixed vegetables

In a large saucepan, cook beef over medium heat until no longer pink; drain. Stir in the V8 juice, dry soup mix, contents of noodle seasoning packet and mixed vegetables. Bring to a boil. Reduce heat; simmer, uncovered, for 6 minutes or until vegetables are tender. Return to a boil; stir in noodles. Cook for 3 minutes or until noodles are tender. **Yield:** 8 servings.

Heartwarming Chili

"Loaded with both beef and pork, this soup is extra meaty," notes Christine Panzarella of Buena Park, California. *"I keep it mild so it's easy on sensitive stomachs and for children who can't handle hot spices. Sometimes, I make the chili without beans and serve it on hot dogs, as a base for burritos or over white rice for a main dish."*

1 pound ground beef
1 pound ground pork
1 medium onion, chopped
½ cup chopped green pepper
1½–2 cups water
1 can (15 ounces) tomato sauce
1 can (15 ounces) pinto beans, rinsed and drained
1 can (14½ ounces) diced tomatoes, undrained
1 envelope chili seasoning
¼ teaspoon garlic salt
Shredded cheddar cheese, sour cream, chopped green onions *and/or* hot pepper slices, optional

In a large saucepan or Dutch oven, cook beef, pork, onion and green pepper over medium heat until meat is no longer pink and vegetables are tender; drain. Add the water, tomato sauce, beans, tomatoes, chili seasoning and garlic salt. Bring to a boil. Reduce heat; simmer, uncovered, until heated through. Garnish with cheese, sour cream, green onions and/or hot peppers if desired. **Yield:** 8–10 servings.

Baked Bean Chili

"Who says a good chili has to simmer all day?" asks Nancy Wall of Bakersfield, California. "This zippy chili can be made on the spur of the moment. It's an excellent standby when unexpected guests drop in. Served with bread and a salad, it's a hearty dinner everyone raves about."

2 pounds ground beef
3 cans (28 ounces *each*) baked beans
1 can (46 ounces) tomato juice
1 can (11½ ounces) V8 juice
1 envelope chili seasoning

In a Dutch oven, cook beef over medium heat until no longer pink; drain. Stir in the remaining ingredients. Bring to a boil. Reduce heat; simmer, uncovered, for 10 minutes. **Yield:** 24 servings.

Hearty Hamburger Soup

"This thick soup, chock-full of veggies and noodles, satisfies my husband's appetite after a busy day on the farm," reports Julie Green of Hull, Iowa. "It's especially handy for us to make because we raise our own beef."

2 pounds ground beef
½ cup chopped onion
6 cups water
1 package (10 ounces) frozen mixed vegetables
1 can (14½ ounces) diced tomatoes, undrained
1 package (6¾ ounces) beef pasta dinner mix
1 bay leaf
¼–½ teaspoon salt
¼ teaspoon pepper

In a Dutch oven or soup kettle, cook the beef and onion over medium heat until meat is no longer pink; drain. Stir in the remaining ingredients; bring to a boil. Reduce heat; cover and simmer until pasta is tender. Discard bay leaf before serving. **Yield:** 12 servings.

Broccoli Wild Rice Soup

"My daughter relies on a boxed rice mix to get a head start on this rich and colorful soup," reports Janet Sawyer of Dysart, Iowa. *"She likes to serve it to friends after football games in autumn, but it's a favorite with our family anytime of year."*

1 package (6 ounces) chicken and wild rice mix
5 cups water
1 package (10 ounces) frozen chopped broccoli, thawed
1 medium carrot, shredded
2 teaspoons dried minced onion
1 can (10¾ ounces) condensed cream of chicken soup, undiluted
1 package (8 ounces) cream cheese, cubed
¼ cup slivered almonds, optional

In a large saucepan, combine rice, contents of seasoning packet and water; bring to a boil. Reduce heat; cover and simmer for 10 minutes, stirring once. Stir in the broccoli, carrot and onion. Cover and simmer for 5 minutes. Stir in soup and cream cheese. Cook and stir until cheese is melted. Stir in almonds if desired. **Yield:** 8 servings (about 2 quarts).

Beefy Tomato Soup

Ground beef and macaroni add heartiness to this soup by Patricia Staudt of Marble Rock, Iowa. It's nicely seasoned…and a snap to prepare.

1 pound ground beef
1 quart tomato juice
3 cups water
¾ cup uncooked elbow macaroni
1 envelope onion soup mix
¼ teaspoon chili powder

In a large saucepan, cook beef over medium heat until no longer pink; drain. Add the remaining ingredients. Bring to a boil. Reduce heat; simmer, uncovered, for 15–20 minutes or until macaroni is tender. **Yield:** 8 servings.

Vegetable Noodle Soup

"This creamy soup is great on a cold winter day," assures Judie Peters of Camden, Indiana. *"I created it when I didn't have all the ingredients for broccoli soup. I like this combo even better."*

3½ cups milk
1 package (16 ounces) frozen California-blend vegetables
½ cup cubed process American cheese
1 envelope chicken noodle soup mix

In a large saucepan, bring milk to a boil. Stir in vegetables and return to a boil. Reduce heat; cover and simmer for 6 minutes. Stir in cheese and soup mix. Return to a boil. Reduce heat. Simmer, uncovered, for 5–7 minutes or until the noodles are tender and the cheese is melted, stirring occasionally. **Yield:** 5–6 servings.

Slow-Cooked Chunky Chili

"Pork sausage, ground beef and plenty of beans make this chili a hearty meal-starter", says Margie Shaw of Greenbrier, Arkansas. *"I keep the versatile mixture in serving-size containers in my freezer at all times. I can quickly warm up bowls of it on cold days."*

1 pound ground beef
1 pound bulk pork sausage
4 cans (16 ounces *each*) kidney beans, rinsed and drained
2 cans (14-½ ounces *each*) diced tomatoes, undrained
2 cans (10 ounces *each*) diced tomatoes and green chilies, undrained
1 large onion, chopped
1 medium green pepper, chopped
1 envelope taco seasoning
½ teaspoon salt
¼ teaspoon pepper

In a skillet, cook beef and sausage over medium heat until meat is no longer pink; drain. Transfer to a 5-qt. slow cooker. Stir in the remaining ingredients. Cover and cook on high for 4–5 hours or until vegetables are tender. Serve desired amount. Cool the remaining chili; transfer to freezer bags or containers. Freeze for up to 3 months. **To use frozen chili:** Thaw in the refrigerator; place in a saucepan and heat through. Add water if desired. **Yield:** 12 servings (3 quarts).

Smoked Sausage Soup

"Whenever I serve this thick stew-like soup to new friends, they never fail to ask for the recipe," reports Marge Wheeler of San Benito, Texas. Each satisfying bowl is chock-full of tasty smoked sausage, hash browns, green beans, carrots and more.

4½ cups water
1 can (28 ounces) diced tomatoes, undrained
1 envelope onion soup mix
1 package (9 ounces) frozen cut green beans
3 small carrots, halved and thinly sliced
2 celery ribs, thinly sliced
1 tablespoon sugar
½ teaspoon salt
½ teaspoon dried oregano
⅛ teaspoon hot pepper sauce
1 pound fully cooked smoked sausage, halved and thinly sliced
2½ cups frozen shredded hash brown potatoes

In a soup kettle or Dutch oven, combine the first 10 ingredients. Bring to a boil. Reduce heat; cover and simmer for 20–25 minutes or until the vegetables are tender. Stir in the sausage and hash browns. Bring to a boil. Reduce heat; cover and cook for 5 minutes or until heated through. **Yield:** 12 servings.

Sausage Stroganoff Soup

Helen Haviland of Greenfield, Illinois starts this rich soup with handy scalloped potato mix and brown-and-serve breakfast sausages. "It's not your ordinary potato soup," she assures.

1 package (12 ounces) brown-and-serve sausage links, cut into ½-inch slices
1 garlic clove, minced
1 package (5 ounces) scalloped potatoes
3 cups water
1 can (14½ ounces) chicken broth
1 jar (4½ ounces) sliced mushrooms, drained
1 cup half-and-half cream
1 cup (8 ounces) sour cream
2 tablespoons Dijon mustard
Paprika, optional

In a large saucepan, cook sausage and garlic until sausage is lightly browned, about 6 minutes. Stir in the contents of the potato and sauce packets. Add water, broth and mushrooms. Bring to a boil. Reduce heat; simmer, uncovered, for 14–16 minutes or until potatoes are tender. Stir in the cream, sour cream and mustard; heat through (do not boil). Sprinkle with paprika if desired. **Yield:** 6–8 servings.

CHAPTER 6

Breads

Parmesan Herb Bread

"Wedges of this delicious cheese-topped bread go great with spaghetti and other Italian dishes," notes Diane Hixon of Niceville, Florida. *"They also taste special when dressed up with one of these flavorful spreads."*

1½ cups biscuit/baking mix
1 egg, beaten
¼ cup apple juice
¼ cup milk
1 tablespoon dried minced onion
1 tablespoon sugar
½ teaspoon dried oregano
¼ cup grated Parmesan cheese

HERB BUTTER:
½ cup butter, softened
1 garlic clove, minced
2 tablespoons minced fresh parsley *or* 2 teaspoons dried parsley flakes
1 teaspoon dried basil

TOMATO BUTTER:
½ cup butter, softened
4 teaspoons tomato paste
Dash cayenne pepper

In a mixing bowl, combine the first seven ingredients just until blended. Spoon into a greased 9-in. round baking pan. Sprinkle with Parmesan cheese. Bake at 400° for 18–20 minutes or until golden brown. In separate small mixing bowls, combine herb butter and tomato butter ingredients; beat until smooth. Serve with warm bread. **Yield:** 6–8 servings.

Gumdrop Bread

Colorful gumdrops make these fun miniature loaves just perfect for holiday gift-giving. "I usually bake this moist bread at Christmas, but it's also requested at Easter," notes Linda Samaan of Fort Wayne, Indiana.

3 cups biscuit/baking mix
⅔ cup sugar
1 egg
1¼ cups milk
1½ cups chopped nuts
1 cup chopped gumdrops

In a bowl, combine biscuit mix and sugar. In another bowl, beat the egg and milk; add to dry ingredients and stir well. Add nuts and gumdrops; stir just until mixed. Pour into three greased 5¾-in. × 3-in. × 2-in. loaf pans. Bake at 350° for 35 minutes or until a toothpick inserted near the center comes out clean. Cool for 10 minutes; remove from pans to wire racks to cool completely. **Yield:** 3 mini loaves.

Broccoli-Cheese Corn Bread

This moist corn bread, which relies on convenient muffin mix and frozen broccoli, is a breeze to whip up anytime. "It's especially good in the winter with a steaming bowl of soup," relates Charlotte McDaniel of Anniston, Alabama.

4 eggs
½ cup butter, melted
¾ teaspoon salt
1 package (8½ ounces) corn bread/muffin mix
1 package (10 ounces) frozen chopped broccoli, thawed and drained
1 cup (4 ounces) shredded cheddar cheese
1 medium onion, chopped

In a bowl, combine eggs, butter and salt. Stir in corn bread mix just until blended. Stir in the remaining ingredients. Pour into a greased 11-in. × 7-in. × 2-in. baking pan. Bake at 350° for 30–35 minutes or until a toothpick inserted near the center comes out clean. Slice and serve warm. **Yield:** 12 servings. **Editor's Note:** To make muffins instead of bread, fill greased muffin cups three-fourths full. Bake at 350° for 20–25 minutes or until a toothpick comes out clean. **Yield:** 1½ dozen.

Fiesta Bread

"A neighbor gave me this quick-and-easy recipe more than 25 years ago, when my children were small," recalls Helen Carpenter of Highland Haven, Texas. *"You can use your favorite seasoning mix in this bread, so it's very versatile."*

2 cups biscuit/baking mix
⅔ cup milk
4½ teaspoons chili seasoning
2 tablespoons butter, melted

In a bowl, combine the biscuit mix, milk and seasoning; mix well. Pat into a greased 8-in. baking pan; drizzle with butter. Bake at 425° for 15–17 minutes or until a toothpick inserted near the center comes out clean. **Yield:** 9 servings. **Editor's Note:** Italian or ranch salad dressing mix, taco seasoning or onion soup mix may be substituted for the chili seasoning.

Sunshine Muffins

Linnea Rein of Topeka, Kansas uses two convenient mixes to create these sweet corn bread muffins. The yellow cake mix gives them a smoother texture than traditional corn bread.

2 eggs
½ cup water
⅓ cup milk
2 tablespoons vegetable oil
1 package (9 ounces) yellow cake mix
1 package (8½ ounces) corn bread/muffin mix

In a bowl, combine the eggs, water, milk and oil. Stir in mixes and mix well. Fill greased and floured muffin cups half full. Bake at 350° for 18–22 minutes or until a toothpick comes out clean. Cool for 5 minutes; remove from pans to wire racks. **Yield:** 14 muffins.

Mini Cheddar Loaves

It's hard to believe you need only four ingredients to bake up a batch of these beautiful miniature loaves. "Sliced warm from the oven, this golden bread is simple and delicious," notes Melody Rowland of Chattanooga, Tennessee.

3½ **cups biscuit/baking mix**
2½ **cups (10 ounces) shredded sharp cheddar cheese**
  2 **eggs**
1¼ **cups milk**

In a large bowl, combine biscuit mix and cheese. Beat eggs and milk; stir into cheese mixture just until moistened. Pour into four greased and floured 5¾-in. × 3-in. × 2-in. loaf pans. Bake at 350° for 35–40 minutes or until a toothpick inserted near the center comes out clean. Cool for 10 minutes. Remove from pans; slice and serve warm. **Yield:** 4 mini loaves. **Editor's Note:** Bread can also be made in one 9-in. × 5-in. × 3-in. loaf pan. Bake for 50–55 minutes.

Ranch Garlic Bread

"I've worked as a manager of a fast-food restaurant for 12 years," relates John Palmer of Cottonwood, California. *"At home, I like to cook using everyday ingredients."* John gives a loaf of French bread plenty of flavor simply with salad dressing mix and garlic powder.

1 cup butter, softened
2–3 tablespoons ranch salad dressing mix
2 teaspoons garlic powder
1 loaf (1 pound) French bread, halved lengthwise

In a small mixing bowl, combine butter, dressing mix and garlic powder; beat until combined. Spread over cut sides of bread. Place on a baking sheet. Broil 4–6 in. from the heat for 3–4 minutes or until golden brown. **Yield:** 8 servings.

Tex-Mex Biscuits

"I love cooking with green chilies because they add so much flavor to ordinary dishes," notes Angie Trolz of Jackson, Michigan. *"Once while making a pot of chili, I had some green chilies left over and mixed them into my biscuit dough, creating this recipe. These fresh-from-the-oven treats are a wonderful accompaniment to soup or chili."*

2 cups biscuit/baking mix
⅔ cup milk
1 cup (4 ounces) finely shredded cheddar cheese
1 can (4 ounces) chopped green chilies, drained

In a bowl, combine biscuit mix and milk until a soft dough forms. Stir in cheese and chilies. Turn onto a floured surface; knead 10 times. Roll out to ½-in. thickness; cut with a 2½-in. biscuit cutter. Place on an ungreased baking sheet. Bake at 450° for 8–10 minutes or until golden brown. Serve warm. **Yield:** about 1 dozen.

Green Chili Corn Muffins

"While visiting a local Mexican restaurant, I sampled a spicy corn muffin with a surprising sweetness," explains Melissa Cook of Chico, California. *"This recipe is a result of numerous attempts to re-create that treat using convenient mixes. These moist muffins are tasty with Mexican dishes, chili and soup."*

1 package (8½ ounces) corn bread/muffin mix
1 package (9 ounces) yellow cake mix
2 eggs
½ cup milk
⅓ cup water
2 tablespoons vegetable oil
1 can (4 ounces) chopped green chilies, drained
1 cup (4 ounces) shredded cheddar cheese, *divided*

In a bowl, combine dry corn bread and cake mixes. In another bowl, combine the eggs, milk, water and oil. Stir into the dry ingredients just until moistened. Add chilies and ¾ cup cheese. Fill greased or paper-lined muffin cups two-thirds full. Bake at 350° for 20–22 minutes or until muffins test done. Immediately sprinkle with remaining cheese. Cool for 5 minutes before removing from pans to wire racks. Serve warm. **Yield:** 16 servings.

Bacon Cheddar Muffins

Cheddar cheese and bacon add hearty flavor to these tasty muffins from Suzanne McKinley of Lyons, Georgia. Calling for just six ingredients, they're quick to stir up and handy to eat on the run.

2 cups biscuit/baking mix
⅔ cup milk
¼ cup vegetable oil
1 egg
1 cup (4 ounces) finely shredded sharp cheddar cheese
8 bacon strips, cooked and crumbled

In a bowl, combine biscuit mix, milk, oil and egg just until moistened. Fold in cheese and bacon. Fill greased muffin cups three-fourths full. Bake at 375° for 20 minutes or until golden brown. Cool for 10 minutes; remove from pan to a wire rack. **Yield:** about 1 dozen.

Onion Rye Breadsticks

An envelope of onion soup mix provides the fast flavor you'll find in these rye snacks from Barbara Brown of Kentwood, Michigan. "They're an easy accompaniment to soup or salad when time's at a premium," she notes.

½ cup butter, softened
1 envelope onion soup mix
14 slices rye bread

Combine butter and soup mix; spread over bread. Cut each slice into ¾-in. strips and place on ungreased baking sheets. Bake at 350° for 5–6 minutes or until butter is melted and breadsticks are crisp. **Yield:** about 7 dozen.

Onion Sandwich Rolls

"These tempting rolls have a mild onion flavor thanks to dry soup mix," notes Josie-Lynn Belmont of Woodbine, Georgia. "They are great with Italian meals or as sandwich rolls or hamburger buns. Plus, they freeze well."

1 envelope onion soup mix
½ cup boiling water
1 tablespoon butter
3½ to 4 cups all-purpose flour, *divided*
2 packages (¼ ounce *each*) quick-rise yeast
1 tablespoon sugar
1 cup warm water (120° to 130°)

In a bowl, combine soup mix, boiling water and butter; cool to 120°–130°. In a mixing bowl, combine 1 cup flour, yeast and sugar. Add warm water; beat until smooth. Stir in 1 cup flour. Beat in onion soup mixture and enough remaining flour to form a soft dough. Turn onto a floured surface; knead until smooth and elastic, about 6 minutes. Cover and let stand for 10 minutes. Divide dough into 12 portions and shape each into a ball. Place on greased baking sheets; flatten slightly. Place two large shallow pans on the work surface; fill half full with boiling water. Place baking pans with rolls over water-filled pans. Cover and let rise for 15 minutes. Bake at 375° for 16–19 minutes or until golden brown. Remove from pans to a wire rack. **Yield:** 1 dozen.

Poppy Seed Biscuits

In her Emerald Park, Saskatchewan home, Diane Molberg uses convenient baking mix to stir up these pleasant-tasting biscuits. "The subtly sweet seeded treats are a good accompaniment to soup or a main-dish salad," she assures.

    ¼ cup milk
    2 tablespoons honey
    ½ cup cream-style cottage cheese
 2¼ cups biscuit/baking mix
    1 tablespoon poppy seeds

In a blender, combine milk, honey and cottage cheese. Cover and process until smooth. In a bowl, combine biscuit mix and poppy seeds. Stir in cottage cheese mixture just until blended. Turn onto a floured surface; pat or knead to ½-in. thickness. Cut with a 2½-in. biscuit cutter. Place on an ungreased baking sheet. Bake at 425° for 8–10 minutes or until golden brown. **Yield:** about 1 dozen.

Cheddar Sausage Muffins

Handy biscuit mix and cheese soup hurry along these hearty muffins from Melissa Vannoy of Childress, Texas. The golden muffins are great with soup at lunch.

    1 pound bulk pork sausage
    1 can (10¾ ounces) condensed cheddar cheese soup, undiluted
    1 cup (4 ounces) shredded cheddar cheese
 ⅔ cup water
    3 cups biscuit/baking mix

In a skillet over medium heat, cook sausage until no longer pink; drain. In a bowl, combine soup, cheese and water. Stir in biscuit mix until blended. Add sausage. Fill greased muffin cups three-fourths full. Bake at 350° for 20–25 minutes or until a toothpick comes out clean. Cool for 5 minutes before removing from pans to wire racks. Serve warm. **Yield:** about 1½ dozen.

Mini Cheese Biscuits

"To complete a meal, I pass a basket of these biscuits," says Chris Rentmeister of Ripon, Wisconsin. *"We're garlic lovers, so we enjoy the flavor of these easy biscuits. If your taste buds prefer, omit the minced garlic altogether. Friends and family tell me these treats are best warm from the oven."*

2 cups biscuit/baking mix
½ cup shredded cheddar cheese
2 garlic cloves, minced
⅔ cup milk
2 tablespoons butter, melted
¼ teaspoon garlic powder

In a bowl, combine biscuit mix, cheese and garlic. With a fork, stir in milk just until moistened. Drop by rounded tablespoonfuls onto a lightly greased baking sheet. Bake at 450° for 9–11 minutes or until golden brown. Combine butter and garlic powder; brush over biscuits. **Yield:** about 1 dozen.

Barbecued Olive Bread

"We cook on the grill all year long, so this zesty olive-topped bread accompanies everything from pork to beef to chicken," notes Patricia Gasper of Peoria, Illinois. *"It also makes a tempting appetizer."*

1 can (4½ ounces) chopped ripe olives, drained
½ cup chopped stuffed olives
¾ cup shredded Colby/Monterey Jack cheese
¾ cup grated Parmesan cheese, *divided*
¼ cup butter, melted
1 tablespoon olive oil
2 garlic cloves, minced
3 drops hot pepper sauce
2 cups biscuit/baking mix
⅔ cup milk
2 tablespoons minced fresh parsley
Paprika

In a bowl, combine the olives, Colby/Monterey Jack cheese, ½ cup Parmesan cheese, butter, oil, garlic and hot pepper sauce; set aside. In another bowl, combine biscuit mix, milk, 2 tablespoons Parmesan cheese and parsley just until moistened. Press into two greased 9-in. disposable aluminum pie pans. Top with olive mixture; sprinkle with paprika and remaining Parmesan. Grill bread, covered, over indirect heat for 8–10 minutes or until bottom crust is golden brown when edge of bread is lifted with a spatula. **Yield:** 2 loaves (6–8 servings each).

Round Cheese Bread

From Medicine Hat, Alberta, Deborah Bitz shares this savory round loaf with Italian flair. "Warm buttered wedges are tasty with a pasta dinner or tossed salad," she informs.

1½ cups biscuit/baking mix
1 cup (4 ounces) shredded mozzarella cheese
¼ cup grated Parmesan cheese
½ teaspoon dried oregano
½ cup milk
1 egg, beaten
2 tablespoons butter, melted
Additional Parmesan cheese

In a bowl, combine the first six ingredients (batter will be thick). Spoon into a greased 8-in. round baking pan. Drizzle with butter; sprinkle with additional Parmesan cheese. Bake at 400° for 20–25 minutes or until a toothpick inserted near the center comes out clean. Cool for 10 minutes. Cut into wedges. Serve warm. **Yield:** 6–8 servings.

Ginger Biscuits

From Mechanicsville, Maryland, Elaine Green shares the recipe for mildly spiced biscuits that taste best served warm. They rely on convenient baking mix and orange yogurt, so they're virtually fuss-free.

3 cups reduced-fat biscuit/ baking mix
3 tablespoons sugar
½ teaspoon ground ginger
2 tablespoons cold margarine
1 carton (6 ounces) reduced-fat orange yogurt
¼ cup plus 1 tablespoon egg substitute, *divided*

In a bowl, combine the biscuit mix, sugar and ginger. Cut in margarine until the mixture resembles coarse crumbs. With a fork, stir in yogurt and ¼ cup egg substitute until mixture forms a ball. Turn onto a floured surface; knead 5–6 times. Roll out to ½-in. thickness; cut with a 2½-in. biscuit cutter. Place on an ungreased baking sheet. Brush tops with remaining egg substitute. Bake at 425° for 14–16 minutes or until golden brown. **Yield:**16 biscuits.

Italian Seasoned Bread

"When I didn't have the onion soup mix called for in the original recipe, I used Italian salad dressing mix instead," writes Jill Dickinson of Aurora, Minnesota. "Now this mildly seasoned bread is my family's favorite."

1 cup plus 3 tablespoons water (70° to 80°)
4½ teaspoons butter
½ teaspoon salt
1 envelope zesty Italian salad dressing mix
1 tablespoon sugar
3 cups bread flour
4½ teaspoons nonfat dry milk powder
2¼ teaspoons active dry yeast

In bread machine pan, place all ingredients in order suggested by manufacturer. Select basic bread setting. Choose crust color and loaf size if available. Bake according to bread machine directions (check dough after 5 minutes of mixing; add 1 to 2 tablespoons of water or flour if needed). **Yield:** 1 loaf (1½ pounds, 16 slices).

Cheddar Zucchini Wedges

In Camano Island, Washington, Vevie Clarke stirs together convenient biscuit mix, tender zucchini, cheddar cheese and toasted almonds to create this flavorful round bread. The golden wedges look as appealing as they taste.

1 medium onion, chopped
¼ cup butter
2½ cups biscuit/baking mix
1 tablespoon minced fresh parsley
½ teaspoon dried basil
½ teaspoon dried thyme
3 eggs, beaten
¼ cup milk
1½ cups shredded zucchini
1 cup (4 ounces) shredded cheddar cheese
¾ cup chopped almonds, toasted

In a skillet, saute onion in butter until tender. In a bowl, combine the biscuit mix, parsley, basil, thyme and onion mixture. Stir in eggs and milk just until combined. Fold in the zucchini, cheese and almonds. Transfer to a greased 9-in. round baking pan. Bake at 400° for 25–30 minutes or until a toothpick inserted near the center comes out clean. Cut into wedges. **Yield:** 6–8 servings.

Corn Bread Strips

"I discovered this recipe over 30 years ago and have used it ever since," remarks Patricia Kile of Greentown, Pennsylvania. With just three ingredients, the corn-flavored strips couldn't be simpler.

2 cups biscuit/baking mix
1 can (8½ ounces) cream-style corn
3 tablespoons butter, melted

In a bowl, combine biscuit mix and corn until mixture forms a ball. Turn onto a lightly floured surface and knead 10–12 times. Pat into a 10-in. × 6-in. rectangle. Cut into 3-in. × 1-in. strips; roll in butter. Place in a greased 15-in. × 10-in. × 1-in. baking pan. Bake at 450° for 12–14 minutes or until golden brown. Serve warm. **Yield:** 20 strips.

Mexican Sunset Bread

"I always serve this tasty taco-seasoned bread with chili or cream soups," remarks Bobbie Hruska of Montgomery, Minnesota. "With its slightly chewy crust and wonderful texture inside, I'm sure you'll love it, too."

⅔ cup water (70° to 80°)
½ cup sour cream
3 tablespoons chunky salsa
2 tablespoons plus 1½ teaspoons taco seasoning
4½ teaspoons sugar
1½ teaspoons dried parsley flakes
1 teaspoon salt
3⅓ cups bread flour
1½ teaspoons active dry yeast

In bread machine pan, place all ingredients in order suggested by manufacturer. Select basic bread setting. Choose crust color and loaf size if available. Bake according to bread machine directions (check dough after 5 minutes of mixing; add 1 to 2 tablespoons of water or flour if needed). **Yield:** 1 loaf (about 2 pounds). **Editor's Note:** If your bread machine has a timer feature, we recommend you do not use it for this recipe.

Herb Garlic Loaf

"Everyone who tastes this savory bread wants the recipe," reports Juanita Patterson of Quartzsite, Arizona. "With its mild garlic seasoning, slices of it are excellent with spaghetti, chili, stew or soup."

1 cup plus 2 tablespoons water (70° to 80°)
4½ teaspoons butter, softened
½ teaspoon salt
3 cups bread flour
1 envelope savory herb with garlic soup mix
4½ teaspoons nonfat dry milk powder
1 tablespoon sugar
2¼ teaspoons active dry yeast

In a bread machine pan, place all ingredients in order suggested by manufacturer. Select basic bread setting. Choose crust color and loaf size if available. Bake according to bread machine directions (check dough after 5 minutes of mixing; add 1 to 2 tablespoons of water or flour if needed). **Yield:** 1 loaf (1½ pounds, 16 slices).

Corn Dog Muffins

"Our three boys were always asking for corn dogs, so I came up with this fast way to deliver the same flavor," explains Lynita Arteberry of Plankinton, South Dakota. These sweet corn bread muffins, chock-full of hot dog chunks and corn kernels, taste just like the real thing.

2 packages (8½ ounces *each*) corn bread/muffin mix
2 tablespoons brown sugar
2 eggs
1 cup milk
1 can (11 ounces) whole kernel corn, drained
5 hot dogs, chopped

In a bowl, combine corn bread mix and brown sugar. Combine eggs and milk; stir into dry ingredients until moistened. Stir in corn and hot dogs (batter will be thin). Fill greased or paper-lined muffin cups three-fourths full. Bake at 400° for 14–18 minutes or until golden brown. Serve immediately or refrigerate. **Yield:** 1½ dozen.

Ranch Hamburger Buns

"The dough setting on my bread machine makes it easy to prepare fresh rolls in a variety of shapes," relates Nancy Whitney of Seattle, Washington. *"We especially like these hamburger buns that are golden, tender and flavorful."*

½ cup water (70° to 80°)
½ cup plain yogurt
1 egg
¾ cup shredded cheddar cheese
2 tablespoons nonfat dry milk powder
4½ teaspoons sugar
1 tablespoon ranch salad dressing mix
1½ teaspoons salt
3 cups bread flour
2¼ teaspoons active dry yeast

EGG WASH:
1 egg
2 tablespoons water
Poppy seeds *or* sesame seeds, optional

In bread machine pan, place the first 10 ingredients in order suggested by manufacturer. Select dough setting (check dough after 5 minutes of mixing; add 1 to 2 tablespoons of water or flour if needed). When the cycle is completed, turn dough onto a lightly greased surface. Cut into 12 pieces; shape each into a round ball. Place in greased jumbo muffin cups or 4½-in. disposable aluminum foil pans. (If using foil pans, place on two baking sheets.) Cover and let rise in a warm place until doubled, about 45 minutes. Meanwhile, whisk together egg and water. Brush over buns; sprinkle with poppy or sesame seeds if desired. Bake at 400° for 8–12 minutes or until lightly browned. Remove from pans to wire racks to cool. **Yield:** 1 dozen. **Editor's Note:** If your bread machine has a timer feature, we recommend you do not use it for this recipe.

CHAPTER 7

Cakes, Cookies
& Bars

Quick Little Devils

Enjoy the classic combination of peanut butter and chocolate in these speedy squares from Denise Smith of Lusk, Wyoming. A short list of ingredients, including devil's food cake mix, yields chocolaty results that are sure to satisfy any sweet tooth.

1 package (18¼ ounces) devil's food cake mix
1 cup butter, melted
1 jar (7 ounces) marshmallow creme
¾ cup peanut butter

In a bowl, combine cake mix and butter; mix well. Set aside 1 cup for topping. Spread remaining cake mixture into a greased 13-in. × 9-in. × 2-in. baking pan. Combine the marshmallow creme and peanut butter; carefully spread over cake mixture. Crumble reserved cake mixture over the top. Bake at 350° for 18–20 minutes or until a toothpick inserted near the center comes out with moist crumbs (do not overbake). Cool completely. Cut into squares. **Yield:** about 2½ dozen.

Coconut Chip Cookies

Flora Alers of Clinton, Maryland transforms a boxed white cake mix into a big batch of tasty cookies that are filled with coconut, nuts and chocolate chips. "This recipe requires just six ingredients, so you can mix up the batter in a jiffy," she notes.

1 package (18¼ ounces) white cake mix
2 eggs
⅓ cup vegetable oil
1 cup flaked coconut
½ cup semisweet chocolate chips
¼ cup chopped macadamia nuts *or* almonds

In a mixing bowl, beat cake mix, eggs and oil (batter will be very stiff). Stir in coconut, chips and nuts. Roll into 1-in. balls. Place on lightly greased baking sheets. Bake at 350° for 10 minutes or until a slight indentation remains when lightly touched. Cool for 2 minutes; remove to a wire rack to cool completely. **Yield:** 3½ dozen.

White Chocolate Fudge Cake

"This sweet cake, with its thick frosting and rich chocolate layer, is a big hit at office potlucks," informs Denise VonStein of Shiloh, Ohio. "I have one co-worker who tells everyone it's awful so he can have it all to himself!"

1 package (18¼ ounces) white cake mix
1¼ cups water
3 egg whites
⅓ cup vegetable oil
1 teaspoon vanilla extract
3 squares (1 ounce *each*) white baking chocolate, melted

FILLING:
¾ cup semisweet chocolate chips
2 tablespoons butter

FROSTING:
1 can (16 ounces) vanilla frosting
3 squares (1 ounce *each*) white baking chocolate, melted
1 teaspoon vanilla extract
1 carton (8 ounces) frozen whipped topping, thawed

In a mixing bowl, combine the cake mix, water, egg whites, oil and vanilla. Beat on low for 2 minutes. Stir in white chocolate. Pour into a greased 13-in. × 9-in. × 2-in. baking pan. Bake at 350° for 25–30 minutes or until a toothpick inserted near the center comes out clean. Cool for 5 minutes. Meanwhile, in a microwave or heavy saucepan over low heat, melt chocolate chips and butter; stir until smooth. Carefully spread over warm cake. Cool completely. In a mixing bowl, beat frosting; stir in white chocolate and vanilla. Fold in whipped topping; frost cake. Store in the refrigerator. **Yield:** 16 servings.

Can't-Leave-Alone Bars

Convenient cake mix hurries along the preparation of these tasty bars from Kimberly Biel. "I bring these quick-and-easy treats to church meetings, potlucks and housewarming parties. I often make a double batch so we can enjoy some at home," says the Java, South Dakota cook.

1 package (18¼ ounces) white cake mix
2 eggs
⅓ cup vegetable oil
1 can (14 ounces) sweetened condensed milk
1 cup (6 ounces) semisweet chocolate chips
¼ cup butter, cubed

In a bowl, combine the cake mix, eggs and oil. With floured hands, press two-thirds of the mixture into a greased 13-in. × 9-in. × 2-in. baking pan. Set remaining cake mixture aside. In a microwave-safe bowl, combine the milk, chocolate chips and butter. Microwave, uncovered, on high for 45 seconds; stir. Microwave 45–60 seconds longer or until chips and butter are melted; stir until smooth. Pour over crust. Drop teaspoonfuls of remaining cake mixture over top. Bake at 350° for 20–25 minutes or until lightly browned. Cool before cutting. **Yield:** 3 dozen. **Editor's Note:** This recipe was tested in an 850-watt microwave.

Rhubarb Upside-Down Cake

In Thompson Falls, Montana, Bonnie Krogman uses a boxed cake mix to create this quick and colorful dessert. "I prepare it often in the summer when fresh rhubarb is abundant," she notes. "When I take it to church potlucks, people really clean up the pan fast."

5 cups cut fresh *or* frozen rhubarb (½-inch pieces), thawed and drained
1 package (6 ounces) strawberry gelatin
½ cup sugar
2 cups miniature marshmallows
1 package (18¼ ounces) white *or* yellow cake mix
Whipped topping, optional

Place rhubarb in a greased 13-in. × 9-in. × 2-in. baking pan. Sprinkle with the gelatin, sugar and marshmallows. Prepare cake mix according to package directions; pour batter over marshmallows. Bake at 350° for 50–55 minutes or until a toothpick inserted near the center comes out clean. Cool for 10 minutes; invert cake onto a serving plate. Serve with whipped topping if desired. **Yield:** 12–16 servings.

Pineapple Upside-Down Cake

Anna Polhemus of North Merrick, New York doles out slices of this sunny-colored dessert while it's still warm from the oven. The moist cake gets its fruity flavor from crushed pineapple and lemon gelatin.

1 can (20 ounces) unsweetened crushed pineapple
1 package (.3 ounce) sugar-free lemon gelatin
Egg substitute equivalent to 2 eggs
1 egg white
¾ cup sugar
1 teaspoon vanilla extract
¾ cup all-purpose flour
1 teaspoon baking powder

Drain pineapple, reserving ⅓ cup juice (discard or save for another use). Line a 9-in. round baking pan with waxed paper; coat with nonstick cooking spray. Spread pineapple over waxed paper; sprinkle with gelatin. In a mixing bowl, beat egg substitute and egg white. Beat in sugar, reserved pineapple juice and vanilla. Combine flour and baking powder; add to egg mixture and stir well. Pour over gelatin. Bake at 350° for 25–30 minutes or until a toothpick inserted near the center comes out clean. Cool for 5 minutes; invert onto a serving plate. Serve warm. **Yield:** 10 servings.

Chocolate Cherry Cupcakes

"Inside each of these cupcakes is a fruity surprise!" promises Bertille Cooper of St. Inigoes, Maryland. She starts with a convenient cake mix to produce her special treats.

1 package (18¼ ounces) chocolate cake mix
1⅓ cups water
½ cup vegetable oil
3 eggs
1 can (21 ounces) cherry pie filling
1 can (16 ounces) vanilla frosting

In a mixing bowl, combine cake mix, water, oil and eggs; mix well. Spoon batter by ¼ cupfuls into paper-lined muffin cups. Spoon a rounded teaspoon of pie filling onto the center of each cupcake. Set remaining pie filling aside. Bake at 350° for 20–25 minutes or until a toothpick inserted on an angle toward the center comes out clean. Remove to a wire rack to cool completely. Frost cupcakes; top with one cherry from pie filling. Serve additional pie filling with cupcakes or refrigerate for another use. **Yield:** 2 dozen.

Apple Cream Cake

"This is the first dessert Mom would make when apples were ready to pick," recalls Antoinette Kilhoffer from Ridgway, Pennsylvania. *"One bite of this old-fashioned country cake will have you coming back for more. A boxed cake mix makes it easy, but it tastes like it's made from scratch."*

1 package (18¼ ounces) yellow cake mix
3 cups sliced peeled tart apples
½ cup chopped walnuts
¼ cup sugar
1 teaspoon ground cinnamon
1 cup heavy whipping cream
Whipped cream *or* vanilla ice cream, optional

Prepare cake batter according to package directions; pour into a greased 13-in. × 9-in. × 2-in. baking dish. Combine apples, walnuts, sugar and cinnamon; spoon over batter. Pour cream over the top. Bake at 350° for 60–70 minutes or until a toothpick inserted near the center comes out clean. Serve with whipped cream or ice cream if desired.
Yield: 12–15 servings.

Fun Marshmallow Bars

"These colorful kid-tested treats go fast at bake sales," promises Debbie Brunssen, a mother of six from Randolph, Nebraska. *"A cake mix really cuts the prep time."*

1 package (18¼ ounces) devil's food cake mix
¼ cup butter, melted
¼ cup water
1 egg
3 cups miniature marshmallows
1 cup plain M&M's
½ cup chopped peanuts

In a mixing bowl, combine cake mix, butter, water and egg; mix well. Press into a greased 13-in. × 9-in. × 2-in. baking pan. Bake at 375° for 20–22 minutes or until a toothpick inserted near the center comes out clean. Sprinkle with marshmallows, M&M's and peanuts. Bake 2–3 minutes longer or until the marshmallows begin to melt. Cool on a wire rack before cutting. **Yield:** 3½ dozen.

Coconut Chocolate Cake

This heavenly cake from Elsie Shell of Topeka, Indiana is so rich and gooey you wouldn't guess it starts with a boxed cake mix. "Although I love making cakes from scratch, mixes are so convenient," Elsie informs. *"It's fun to spruce them up with goodies like coconut, almonds and chocolate chips."*

1 package (18¼ ounces) chocolate cake mix
1½ cups evaporated milk, *divided*
1½ cups sugar, *divided*
24 large marshmallows
1 package (14 ounces) flaked coconut
½ cup butter
2 cups (12 ounces) semisweet chocolate chips
½ cup slivered almonds, toasted

Mix cake according to package directions, using a 15-in. × 10-in. × 1-in. baking pan. Bake at 350° for 20 minutes or until a toothpick inserted near the center comes out clean. Meanwhile, in a large saucepan, combine 1 cup milk and 1 cup sugar; bring to a boil, stirring occasionally. Remove from the heat. Add marshmallows and stir until melted. Add coconut and mix well. Spread over cake immediately after baking. Cool for 30 minutes. In a small saucepan, combine butter and remaining milk and sugar; bring to a boil. Remove from the heat; stir in the chocolate chips until melted. Spread over coconut layer; sprinkle with almonds. **Yield:** 16–20 servings.

Apple German Chocolate Cake

"This delectable dessert is perfect to bake when unexpected guests stop by," says Shirley Weaver of Zeeland, Michigan. A boxed cake mix and canned pie filling make the moist snack cake a cinch to put together, while chocolate chips and nuts create the quick-and-easy topping.

1 can (21 ounces) apple pie filling
1 package (18¼ ounces) German chocolate cake mix
3 eggs
¾ cup coarsely chopped walnuts
½ cup miniature semisweet chocolate chips

Place pie filling in a blender; cover and process until the apples are in ¼-in. chunks. Pour into a mixing bowl; add cake mix and eggs. Beat on medium speed for 5 minutes. Pour into a greased 13-in. × 9-in. × 2-in. baking pan. Sprinkle with nuts and chocolate chips. Bake at 350° for 40–45 minutes or until a toothpick inserted near the center comes out clean. Cool completely on a wire rack before cutting. **Yield:** 12–15 servings.

Crisp Walnut Cookies

"This is a terrific way to bake fresh cookies in minutes," assures Alice Walcher of North Fairfield, Ohio. Easy one-bowl preparation results in yummy treats that are crisp and chewy at the same time.

1 package (18¼ ounces) yellow cake mix
2 cups quick-cooking oats
½ cup sugar
1 cup vegetable oil
3 eggs
1½ teaspoons vanilla extract
1 cup finely chopped walnuts

In a mixing bowl, combine the cake mix, oats and sugar. Beat in oil, eggs and vanilla. Stir in walnuts. Drop by rounded teaspoonfuls 2 in. apart onto ungreased baking sheets. Bake at 350° for 12–14 minutes or until lightly browned. Remove to wire racks to cool. **Yield:** 6 dozen.

Crunchy Dessert Bars

"My son-in-law is diabetic and loves these five-ingredient frozen dessert bars," says Shirley Reed of San Angelo, Texas. "With their nutty crunch from Grape Nuts cereal, we think they taste like the inside of a Snickers candy bar."

1 pint sugar-free fat-free ice cream, softened
1 cup reduced-fat whipped topping
½ cup reduced-fat peanut butter
1 package (1 ounce) instant sugar-free butterscotch pudding mix
1 cup Grape Nuts cereal

In a mixing bowl, combine the first four ingredients; beat until smooth. Stir in cereal. Transfer to a foil-lined 8-in. square pan. Cover and freeze for 3–4 hours or until firm. Use foil to lift out of pan; discard foil. Cut into bars. **Yield:** 2 dozen.

Peanut Butter Cookie Cups

"I'm a busy school-teacher and pastor's wife who always looks for shortcuts," relates Kristi Tackett of Banner, Kentucky. "I wouldn't dare show my face at a church dinner or bake sale without these tempting peanut butter treats. They're quick and easy to make and always a hit."

1 package (17½ ounces) peanut butter cookie mix
36 miniature peanut butter cups, unwrapped

Prepare cookie mix according to package directions. Roll the dough into 1-in. balls. Place in greased miniature muffin cups. Press dough evenly onto bottom and up sides of each cup. Bake at 350° for 11–13 minutes or until set. Immediately place a peanut butter cup in each cup; press down gently. Cool for 10 minutes; carefully remove from pans. **Yield:** 3 dozen. **Editor's Note:** 2¼ cups peanut butter cookie dough of your choice can be substituted for the mix.

Layered Chocolate Cake

"It is hard to believe this impressive dessert started with a boxed cake mix," relates Dorothy Monroe of Pocatello, Idaho. Cream cheese in the icing provides the luscious finishing touch.

1 package (18¼ ounces) German chocolate cake mix
1⅓ cups water
3 eggs
⅓ cup vegetable oil
1 package (3 ounces) cook-and-serve vanilla pudding mix
1 teaspoon unflavored gelatin
2 cups milk
1 package (8 ounces) cream cheese, softened
½ cup butter, softened
1 teaspoon vanilla extract
1½ cups confectioners' sugar
3 tablespoons baking cocoa

In a mixing bowl, combine the first four ingredients; mix well. Pour into a greased 15-in. × 10-in. × 1-in. baking pan. Bake at 350° for 23–25 minutes. Cool on a wire rack. In a saucepan, combine pudding mix, gelatin and milk; cook according to package directions for pudding. Cool. Cut cake into three 10-in. × 5-in. rectangles. Place one on a serving platter. Spread with half of the pudding mixture; repeat layers. Top with third layer. In a mixing bowl, beat cream cheese and butter. Add vanilla; mix well. Add sugar and cocoa; beat until smooth. Frost top and sides of cake. Refrigerate until serving. **Yield:** 10 servings.

Chocolate Pudding Cake

From Lawrenceville, Georgia, Paige Arnette sends this recipe for a rich, fudgy dessert that's a cross between pudding and cake. "I like to serve it warm with a scoop of vanilla ice cream," she writes. "Whenever I take it to parties, everybody wants the recipe."

1 package (18¼ ounces) chocolate cake mix
1 package (3.9 ounces) instant chocolate pudding mix
2 cups (16 ounces) sour cream
4 eggs
1 cup water
¾ cup vegetable oil
1 cup (6 ounces) semisweet chocolate chips
Whipped cream *or* vanilla ice cream, optional

In a mixing bowl, combine the first six ingredients. Beat on medium speed for 2 minutes. Stir in chocolate chips. Pour into a 5-qt. slow cooker that has been coated with nonstick cooking spray. Cover and cook on low for 6–7 hours or until a toothpick inserted near the center comes out with moist crumbs. Serve in bowls with whipped cream or ice cream if desired. **Yield:** 10-12 servings.

Coconut Gingerbread Cake

"This unusual dessert came from a little book I bought at a flea market many years ago," explains Paula Hartlett of Mineola, New York. "The broiled orange-coconut topping really dresses up a boxed gingerbread mix. When I bring it to potlucks and family get-togethers, it never lasts long!"

1 package (14½ ounces) gingerbread mix
1 large navel orange
1⅓ cups flaked coconut
½ cup packed brown sugar
2 tablespoons orange juice

Prepare and bake cake according to package directions, using a greased 8-in. square baking pan. Meanwhile, grate 1 tablespoon of peel from the orange; set aside. Peel and section the orange, removing white pith; dice the orange.

When cake tests done, remove from the oven and cool slightly. Combine coconut, brown sugar, orange juice, diced orange and reserved peel; spread over warm cake. Broil 4 in. from the heat for 2–3 minutes or until the top is lightly browned. Cool on a wire rack. **Yield:** 9 servings.

Soft Raisin Cookies

"I modified a recipe for cake mix cookies to make it healthier," relates Ray Amet of Kansas City, Missouri. *"My family likes my version, with its mild spice flavor and touch of sweetness from raisins, even better than the original."*

1 package (9 ounces) yellow cake mix
1 cup quick-cooking oats
6 tablespoons unsweetened applesauce
Egg substitute equivalent to 1 egg
2 tablespoons margarine, melted
½ teaspoon apple pie spice
½ cup raisins

In a mixing bowl, combine the first six ingredients; beat until blended. Stir in raisins. Drop by tablespoonfuls 2 in. apart onto baking sheets coated with nonstick cooking spray. Bake at 375° for 10–12 minutes or until the edges are lightly browned. Cool for 5 minutes before removing to wire racks to cool completely. **Yield:** 2 dozen.

Light Lemon Cake

"I revised a recipe that appeared in the newspaper to come up with this lemony cake topped with a light and creamy frosting," shares Edna Thomas of Warsaw, Indiana. *"Not only is it fast to fix, but it serves a crowd."*

1 package (18¼ ounces) light yellow cake mix
1 package (3.4 ounces) instant lemon pudding mix
1¾ cups water
3 egg whites
¾ cup cold fat-free milk
½ teaspoon lemon extract
1 package (1 ounce) instant sugar-free vanilla pudding mix
1 carton (8 ounces) frozen reduced-fat whipped topping, thawed

In a mixing bowl, combine cake mix, lemon pudding mix, water and egg whites. Beat on low speed for 1 minute. Pour into a 13-in. × 9-in. × 2-in. baking pan coated with nonstick cooking spray. Bake at 350° for 23–28 minutes or until a toothpick inserted near the center comes out clean. Cool. In a mixing bowl, combine milk, extract and vanilla pudding mix. Beat on low for 2 minutes. Fold in whipped topping. Spread over cake. Store in the refrigerator. **Yield:** 20 servings. **Editor's Note:** Sugar-free lemon pudding mix is not available.

Peach Cake

"The first time I made this scrumptious dessert, I was thrilled to find out how easy it was," recalls Donna Britsch of Tega Cay, South Carolina. "Sometimes I'll scoop softened vanilla ice cream on each serving instead of spreading whipped topping over the entire cake."

¾ cup cold butter
1 package (18½ ounces) yellow cake mix
2 egg yolks
2 cups (16 ounces) sour cream
1 can (29 ounces) sliced peaches, drained
½ teaspoon ground cinnamon
1 carton (8 ounces) frozen whipped topping, thawed

In a bowl, cut butter into cake mix until the mixture resembles coarse crumbs. Pat into a greased 13-in. × 9-in. × 2-in. baking pan. In another bowl, beat egg yolks; add the sour cream and mix well. Set aside 6–8 peach slices for garnish. Cut remaining peaches into 1-in. pieces; stir into the sour cream mixture. Spread over crust; sprinkle with cinnamon. Bake at 350° for 25–30 minutes or until the edges begin to brown. Cool on a wire rack. Spread with whipped topping; garnish with reserved peaches. Store in the refrigerator. **Yield:** 12 servings.

Lemon Berry Cake

From Chester, Maryland, Karen Ehatt adds tangy taste to a plain yellow cake mix with lemon gelatin and blueberries. "Serve warm with a dollop of sweet whipped cream," she suggests.

1 package (18¼ ounces) yellow cake mix
1 tablespoon grated lemon peel
2 cups fresh *or* frozen blueberries
1 package (6 ounces) lemon gelatin
1½ cups boiling water
Confectioners' sugar
Whipped cream *or* topping, optional

Prepare cake batter according to package directions. Stir in lemon peel. Pour into a lightly greased 13-in. × 9-in. × 2-in. baking pan. Sprinkle with blueberries. In a bowl, whisk together gelatin and water until gelatin is dissolved. Slowly pour over batter. Bake at 350° for 33–38 minutes or until a toothpick inserted near the center of cake layer comes out with moist crumbs (cake will set upon cooling). Cool slightly on a wire rack. Dust with confectioners' sugar. Serve warm with whipped cream if desired. Store in the refrigerator. **Yield:** 12 servings.

Quick Lemon Angel Food Supreme

An angel food cake mix is dressed up with the addition of lemon peel, lemon extract and a delicious lemon sauce created in the Taste of Home Test Kitchen. It tastes like it's homemade!

1 package (16 ounces) one-step angel food cake mix
2 teaspoons grated lemon peel
½ teaspoon lemon extract

LEMON SAUCE:
   1 can (15¾ ounces) lemon pie filling
3–4 tablespoons milk
   1 tablespoon lemon juice
 ⅛ teaspoon lemon extract
   1 cup whipped topping

Prepare cake batter according to package directions, adding lemon peel and extract. Bake according to package directions. After baking, immediately invert pan and cool completely. For the sauce, combine the pie filling, milk, lemon juice and extract in a mixing bowl; beat until smooth. Fold in whipped topping. Serve with cake. Store sauce in the refrigerator. **Yield:** 12 servings.

Easy German Chocolate Cake

There's no need to frost this yummy chocolate cake from Dawn Glenn of Johnson City, Tennessee. After baking, just turn the cake upside down onto a pretty platter—the coconut and pecan topping is already in place.

1⅓ cups flaked coconut
  1 cup chopped pecans
  1 package (18¼ ounces) German chocolate cake mix
  1 package (8 ounces) cream cheese, softened
 ½ cup butter, softened
  1 egg
  4 cups confectioners' sugar

Sprinkle the coconut and pecans into a greased and floured 13-in. × 9-in. × 2-in. baking pan. Prepare cake mix according to package directions. Pour batter into prepared pan. In a mixing bowl, beat cream cheese and butter until smooth. Add egg and sugar; beat until smooth. Drop by tablespoonfuls over the batter. Carefully spread to within 1 in. of edges. Bake at 325° for 55–60 minutes or until a toothpick inserted near the center comes out clean. Cool for 10 minutes; invert onto a serving plate. **Yield:** 12–16 servings.

Chocolate Creme Cakes

Moist layers of chocolate cake sandwich a sweet and creamy filling in this irresistible recipe shared by Faith Sommers of Beckwourth, California. "The yummy treats are handy to keep in the freezer for lunches and after-school snacks," she notes.

1 package (18¼ ounces) chocolate cake mix
1 package (3.9 ounces) instant chocolate pudding mix
¾ cup vegetable oil
¾ cup water
4 eggs

FILLING:
3 tablespoons all-purpose flour
1 cup milk
½ cup butter, softened
½ cup shortening
1 cup sugar
1 teaspoon vanilla extract

In a mixing bowl, combine cake and pudding mixes, oil, water and eggs; mix well. Pour into a greased and floured 13-in. × 9-in. × 2-in. baking pan. Bake at 350° for 30–35 minutes or until a toothpick inserted near the center comes out clean. Cool for 10 minutes; invert onto a wire rack to cool completely. In a small saucepan, combine flour and milk until smooth. Bring to a boil; cook and stir for 2 minutes or until thickened. Cool. In a mixing bowl, cream the butter, shortening, sugar and vanilla; beat in milk mixture until sugar is dissolved, about 5 minutes. Split cake into two horizontal layers. Spread filling over the bottom layer; cover with top layer. Cut into serving-size pieces. Freeze in an airtight container for up to 1 month. Remove from the freezer 1 hour before serving. **Yield:** 12–18 servings.

Cookie Burgers

You may have to install a drive-thru window in your kitchen after family and friends sample these playful treats from the Hershey Kitchens! Made with a packaged sugar cookie mix and peanut butter chips, the "buns" hold a "patty" of cocoa icing on a bed of green-tinted coconut "lettuce."

DOUGH:
1 package (22.3 ounces) golden sugar cookie mix
2 eggs
⅓ cup vegetable oil
1 teaspoon water
1 package (10 ounces) peanut butter chips, chopped

TOPPING:
¾ cup flaked coconut
5–6 drops green food coloring

FILLING:
½ cup butter, softened
2⅔ cups confectioners' sugar
½ cup baking cocoa
¼ cup milk
1 teaspoon vanilla extract

In a large bowl, combine cookie mix, eggs, oil and water; mix well. Stir in peanut butter chips. Shape into 1¼-in. balls; place 2 in. apart on ungreased baking sheets. Bake at 375° for 9–11 minutes or until lightly browned. Remove to wire racks to cool. Toss coconut and food coloring until coated; set aside. In a mixing bowl, cream butter. Add sugar, cocoa, milk and vanilla; beat until smooth. Frost the bottoms of 22 cookies; sprinkle with coconut. Top with remaining cookies and gently squeeze together. **Yield:** 22 sandwich cookies. **Editor's Note:** You may substitute your favorite sugar cookie recipe for the cookie mix, eggs, oil and water; just add the peanut butter chips.

Caramel Apple Cupcakes

Bring these extra-special cupcakes to your next bake sale and watch how quickly they disappear—if your family doesn't gobble them up first," says Diane Halferty of Corpus Christi, Texas. "Kids will go for the fun appearance and tasty toppings while adults will appreciate the moist spiced cake underneath."

1 package (18¼ ounces) spice *or* carrot cake mix
2 cups chopped peeled tart apples
20 caramels
3 tablespoons milk
1 cup finely chopped pecans, toasted
12 Popsicle sticks

Prepare cake batter according to package directions; fold in apples. Fill 12 greased or paper-lined jumbo muffin cups three-fourths full. Bake at 350° for 20 minutes or until a toothpick comes out clean. Cool for 10 minutes before removing from pans to wire racks to cool completely. In a saucepan, cook the caramels and milk over low heat until smooth. Spread over cupcakes. Sprinkle with pecans. Insert a popsicle stick into the center of each cupcake. **Yield:** 1 dozen.

Berries 'n' Cream Brownies

"If you like chocolate-covered strawberries, you'll love this sweet treat," says New Holland, Pennsylvania's Anna Lapp. "It's an ideal ending to summer meals." A fudgy brownie, whipped topping and fresh fruit make this a no-fuss feast for the eyes as well as the taste buds.

1 package fudge brownie mix (13-inch × 9-inch pan size)
1 carton (8 ounces) frozen whipped topping, thawed
4 cups quartered fresh strawberries
⅓ cup chocolate hard-shell ice cream topping

Prepare and bake brownies according to package directions, using a greased 13-in. × 9-in. × 2-in. baking pan. Cool completely on a wire rack. Spread whipped topping over brownies. Arrange strawberries cut side down over top. Drizzle with chocolate topping. Refrigerate for at least 30 minutes before serving. **Yield:** 12–15 servings.

Giant Spice Cookies

"I heard this cookie recipe over the radio in 1950—shortly after my husband and I married," recalls Sandy Pyeatt of Tacoma, Washington. "The big spicy treats are so nice and chewy, they remain my favorite to this day."

1 package (18¼ ounces) spice cake mix
½ teaspoon ground ginger
¼ teaspoon baking soda
¼ cup water
¼ cup molasses
6 teaspoons vanilla extract

In a bowl, combine the cake mix, ginger and baking soda. Stir in water, molasses and vanilla; mix well. With floured hands, roll into 10 balls. Place 3 in. apart on greased baking sheets; flatten slightly. Bake at 375° for 13–15 minutes or until surface cracks and cookies are firm. Remove to wire racks to cool. **Yield:** 10 cookies.

Brownie Crackles

Chocolate chips and a convenient brownie mix provide the rich chocolate flavor in these sweet cookies from Ellen Govertsen of Wheaton, Illinois. Rolling the dough in powdered sugar gives them their inviting crackled appearance.

1 package fudge brownie mix (13-inch × 9-inch pan size)
1 cup all-purpose flour
1 egg
½ cup water
¼ cup vegetable oil
1 cup (6 ounces) semisweet chocolate chips
Confectioners' sugar

In a mixing bowl, combine brownie mix, flour, egg, water and oil; mix well. Stir in chocolate chips. Place confectioners' sugar in a shallow dish. Drop dough by tablespoonfuls into sugar; roll to coat. Place 2 in. apart on greased baking sheets. Bake at 350° for 8–10 minutes or until set. Remove to wire racks. **Yield:** 4½ dozen.

Mocha Layer Cake

"My family often requests this delightful layer cake," says Terry Gilbert of Orlean, Virginia. "They love the mocha flavor and extra chocolate surprise hidden beneath the taste-tempting frosting."

1 package (18¼ ounces) devil's food or chocolate cake mix
1⅓ cups brewed coffee, room temperature
½ cup vegetable oil
3 eggs
½ cup semisweet chocolate chips

FROSTING:
½ cup butter, softened
½ cup shortening
4 cups confectioners' sugar
¾ cup baking cocoa
¼ teaspoon almond extract
7 tablespoons brewed coffee, room temperature, *divided*
½ cup semisweet chocolate chips

In a mixing bowl, combine cake mix, coffee, oil and eggs; beat on low speed for 30 seconds. Beat on medium for 2 minutes. Pour into two greased and floured 8-in. round cake pans. Bake at 350° for 30–35 minutes or until a toothpick inserted near the center comes out clean. Cool in pans for 5 minutes; invert onto a wire rack. Sprinkle each cake with ¼ cup chocolate chips; when melted, gently spread chocolate over cakes. Place cakes in the freezer. Meanwhile, for frosting, cream butter, shortening and sugar in a mixing bowl. Beat in cocoa and extract. Add 5 tablespoons coffee, 1 tablespoon at a time, beating until light and fluffy. Spread between layers and over the top and sides of cake. In a saucepan, heat chocolate chips and remaining coffee until chocolate is melted; stir until smooth. Pour over cake; carefully spread over the top, allowing it to drizzle down the sides. **Yield:** 10–12 servings. **Editor's Note:** This recipe was tested with Duncan Hines devil's food cake mix.

Chocolate Bundt Cake

In Rockville, Maryland, Jeanine Gould-Kostka knows how to satisfy a chocolate craving in a hurry. "This moist, taste-tempting treat relies on boxed pudding and cake mixes, so it can be stirred up in a jiffy," she relates. "My neighbors can't wait to get this cake for their birthdays each year."

1 package (18¼ ounces) chocolate cake mix
1 package (3.9 ounces) instant chocolate pudding mix
3 tablespoons baking cocoa
1¾ cups milk
2 eggs
2 cups (12 ounces) semisweet chocolate chips
Confectioners' sugar

In a large mixing bowl, combine cake and pudding mixes, cocoa, milk and eggs. Beat on low speed until moistened. Beat on medium for 2 minutes. Stir in the chocolate chips. Pour into a greased and floured 10-in. fluted tube pan. Bake at 350° for 55–60 minutes or until a toothpick inserted near the center comes out clean. Cool for 10 minutes; remove from pan to a wire rack to cool completely. Dust with confectioners' sugar if desired. **Yield:** 12–15 servings.

Butterscotch Chocolate Cake

"This delicious cake can easily be made ahead of time," informs Shelley McKinney of New Castle, Indiana. *"With only four ingredients, it's so simple and yet so good."*

1 package (18¼ ounces) chocolate cake mix
1 jar (17 ounces) butterscotch ice cream topping
1 carton (8 ounces) frozen whipped topping, thawed
3 Butterfinger candy bars (2.1 ounces *each*), coarsely crushed

Prepare and bake cake according to package directions, using a greased 13-in. × 9-in. × 2-in. baking pan. Cool on a wire rack for 30 minutes. Using the end of a wooden spoon handle, poke 12 holes in warm cake. Pour butterscotch topping over cake; cool completely. Spread with whipped topping; sprinkle with candy bars. Refrigerate for at least 2 hours before serving. **Yield:** 12–16 servings.

Cheese-Swirl Chocolate Cake

"I recently made this moist chocolate cake for my sister and her husband," says Jennifer Bangerter of Warrensburg, Missouri. *"I've never seen cake disappear so quickly! It's great with or without the pretty strawberry sauce."*

1 package (8 ounces) cream cheese, softened
4 eggs
¼ cup sugar
½ teaspoon vanilla extract
1 package (18¼ ounces) devil's food cake mix
1¼ cups water
½ cup vegetable oil
1 package (10 ounces) frozen sweetened sliced strawberries, thawed

In a small mixing bowl, combine cream cheese, 1 egg, sugar and vanilla; mix well. Set aside. In a large mixing bowl, combine cake mix, water, oil and remaining eggs. Beat on low speed until moistened; beat on high for 2 minutes. Pour half of the batter into a greased 13-in. × 9-in. × 2-in. baking pan. Drop half of the cream cheese mixture by tablespoonfuls over the batter. Repeat layers. Cut through batter with a knife to swirl the cream cheese mixture. Bake at 350° for 35–40 minutes or until a toothpick inserted near the center comes out clean (cake may crack). Cool on a wire rack. Meanwhile, process strawberries in a blender or food processor until smooth. Serve over cake. **Yield:** 12 servings.

Chewy Date Nut Bars

You'll need just six ingredients, including a convenient boxed cake mix, to bake up these chewy bars chock-full of walnuts and dates from Linda Hutmacher of Teutopolis, Illinois. "They are my husband's favorite snack," she says, "and he loves to take them to work. I often whip up a batch for bake sales or to share with my co-workers at our local car dealership."

1 package (18¼ ounces) yellow cake mix
¾ cup packed brown sugar
¾ cup butter, melted
2 eggs
2 cups chopped dates
2 cups chopped walnuts

In a mixing bowl, combine cake mix and brown sugar. Add butter and eggs; beat on medium speed for 2 minutes. Combine dates and walnuts; stir into batter (the batter will be stiff). Spread into a greased 13-in. × 9-in. × 2-in. baking pan. Bake at 350° for 35–45 minutes or until edges are golden brown. Cool on a wire rack for 10 minutes. Run a knife around sides of pan to loosen; cool completely before cutting. **Yield:** 3 dozen.

Hawaiian Cake

Estella Traeger of Milwaukee, Wisconsin dresses up a boxed yellow cake mix with pineapple, coconut and a delightful blend of instant pudding, cream cheese and whipped topping. "This is a favorite dessert that suits any occasion. Try it once and you're sure to make it again," she promises.

1 package (18¼ ounces) yellow cake mix
2 cups cold milk
2 packages (3.4 ounces *each*) instant vanilla pudding mix
1 package (8 ounces) cream cheese, softened
1 carton (8 ounces) frozen whipped topping, thawed
1 can (20 ounces) crushed pineapple, drained
½ cup chopped maraschino cherries, drained
½ cup flaked coconut
½ cup chopped walnuts

Prepare cake mix according to package directions, using a greased 15-in. × 10-in. × 1-in. baking pan. Bake at 350° for 20–25 minutes or until a toothpick inserted near the center comes out clean; cool completely. In a mixing bowl, combine milk and pudding mixes; beat in cream cheese until smooth. Fold in whipped topping. Spread over cooled cake. Top with the pineapple, cherries, coconut and walnuts. Refrigerate until serving. **Yield:** 16–20 servings.

Raspberry Cake

Marion Anderson of Dalton, Minnesota jazzes up a plain cake with raspberry gelatin and frozen berries. Spread with a light, fruity whipped topping, the festive results make a cool and refreshing dessert.

1 package (18¼ ounces) white cake mix
1 package (3 ounces) raspberry gelatin
1 package (10 ounces) frozen sweetened raspberries, thawed, undrained
4 eggs
½ cup vegetable oil
¼ cup hot water

FROSTING:

1 carton (12 ounces) frozen whipped topping, thawed
1 package (10 ounces) frozen sweetened raspberries, thawed, undrained

In a large bowl, combine cake mix and gelatin powder. Add raspberries with juice, eggs, oil and water. Beat until well blended. Pour into a greased 13-in. × 9-in. × 2-in. baking pan. Bake at 350° for 35–40 minutes or until a toothpick inserted near the center comes out clean. Cool. For frosting, fold whipped topping into raspberries. Spread over cake. Refrigerate for 2 hours before serving. Store in the refrigerator. **Yield:** 12–16 servings.

Peanut Crunch Cake

"Here's a recipe that dresses up a plain old box cake mix," says Sue Smith of Norwalk, Connecticut. "Peanut butter and chocolate chips add fun, yummy flavor to this yellow cake."

1 package (18¼ ounces) yellow cake mix
1 cup peanut butter
½ cup packed brown sugar
1 cup water
3 eggs
¼ cup vegetable oil
½–¾ cup semisweet chocolate chips, *divided*
½–¾ cup peanut butter chips, *divided*
½ cup chopped peanuts

In a mixing bowl, beat cake mix, peanut butter and brown sugar on low speed until crumbly. Set aside ½ cup. Add water, eggs and oil to remaining crumb mixture; blend on low until moistened. Beat on high for 2 minutes. Stir in ¼ cup each chocolate and peanut butter chips. Pour into a greased 13-in. × 9-in. × 2-in. baking pan. Combine peanuts, reserved crumb mixture and the remaining chips; sprinkle over batter. Bake at 350° for 40–45 minutes or until a toothpick inserted near the center comes out clean. Cool completely. **Yield:** 12–16 servings.

Macadamia Chip Cookies

"If you like cookies with a crunch, you'll love these golden treats," promises Dorothy Kollmeyer of Dupo, Illinois. "Crushed peanut brittle adds an unexpected kick to the vanilla chips and brown sugar that flavor the dough. It's hard to believe something this easy to make tastes so terrific."

1 cup butter, softened
¾ cup packed brown sugar
¼ cup sugar
2 eggs
1 teaspoon vanilla extract
2¼ cups all-purpose flour
1 package (3.4 ounces) instant vanilla pudding mix
1 teaspoon baking soda
¼ teaspoon salt
1 package (10 to 12 ounces) vanilla *or* white chips
2 jars (3¼ ounces *each*) macadamia nuts, chopped
½ cup finely crushed peanut brittle

In a mixing bowl, cream butter and sugars until smooth. Add eggs, one at a time, beating well after each addition. Beat in vanilla. Combine the flour, pudding mix, baking soda and salt; gradually add to creamed mixture and mix well. Stir in chips, nuts and peanut brittle. Drop by rounded tablespoonfuls 2 in. apart onto greased baking sheets. Bake at 375° for 10–12 minutes or until golden brown. Remove to wire racks to cool. **Yield:** 5½ dozen.

Rich Butter Cake

"I've been bringing this cake to family get-togethers and church meetings since the 1950s," shares Doris Schloeman of Chicago, Illinois. This scrumptious standby, topped with cream cheese and nuts, can be prepared in a wink.

1 package (16 ounces) pound cake mix
½ cup butter, melted
5 eggs
2 cups confectioners' sugar, *divided*
2 packages (one 8 ounces, one 3 ounces) cream cheese, softened
½ teaspoon vanilla extract
1 cup chopped walnuts

In a large mixing bowl, combine the cake mix, butter and 3 eggs; beat until smooth. Spread into a greased 13-in. × 9-in. × 2-in. baking pan. Set aside 2 tablespoons confectioners' sugar for topping. In a bowl, beat the cream cheese, vanilla, remaining confectioners' sugar and remaining eggs. Pour over batter. Sprinkle with walnuts. Bake at 350° for 35–40 minutes or until cake begins to pull away from sides of pan. Cool on a wire rack. Dust with reserved confectioners' sugar. Store in the refrigerator. **Yield:** 12–15 servings.

German Chocolate Bundt Cake

Chocolate lovers will delight in this moist, rich cake that's easy to prepare using handy mixes and canned frosting. "I only make this dessert if I'm taking it somewhere," reports Nancy Baker of Boonville, Missouri. "I don't want it sitting in my kitchen, where I might be tempted to eat it all!"

1 package (18¼ ounces) yellow cake mix
1 package (3.4 ounces) instant vanilla pudding mix
1 cup (8 ounces) sour cream
3 eggs
½ cup vegetable oil
½ cup water
1 package (4 ounces) German sweet chocolate, grated
1 cup (6 ounces) semisweet chocolate chips
½ cup chopped pecans
½ cup chocolate frosting, melted
Pecan halves

In a mixing bowl, combine cake and pudding mixes, sour cream, eggs, oil and water. Beat on low speed for 2 minutes. Fold in the grated chocolate, chocolate chips and pecans. Transfer to a greased and floured 10-in. fluted tube pan. Bake at 350° for 60–65 minutes or until a toothpick inserted near the center comes out clean. Cool for 10 minutes before removing from pan to a wire rack. Drizzle with frosting; garnish with pecan halves. **Yield:** 12–14 servings.

Creamy Center Cupcakes

"This recipe came from my mother, who made the cake from scratch when I was growing up," recalls Caroline Anderson of Waupaca, Wisconsin. "Sometimes she'd replace the smooth filling with homemade whipped cream."

1 package (18¼ ounces) **devil's food cake mix**
¾ cup **shortening**
⅔ cup **confectioners' sugar**
1 cup **marshmallow creme**
1 teaspoon **vanilla extract**
2 cans (16 ounces *each*) **chocolate frosting**

Prepare and bake cake according to package directions for cupcakes, using paper-lined muffin cups. Cool for 10 minutes before removing from pans to wire racks to cool completely. Meanwhile, in a mixing bowl, cream shortening and sugar. Add marshmallow creme and vanilla; mix well. Insert a very small pastry tip into a pastry or plastic bag; fill with cream filling. Insert tip halfway into the center of each cupcake and fill with a small amount. Frost with chocolate frosting. **Yield:** 2 dozen.

Pear Bundt Cake

Five simple ingredients are all Veronica Ross needs to fix this lovely light dessert. Tiny bits of pear provide sweetness to the moist slices, which she serves in her Columbia Heights, Minnesota home.

1 can (15¼ ounces) **pears in light syrup**
1 package (18¼ ounces) **white cake mix**
2 **egg whites**
1 **egg**
2 teaspoons **confectioners' sugar**

Drain pears, reserving the syrup; chop pears. Place pears and syrup in a mixing bowl; add cake mix, egg whites and egg. Beat on low speed for 30 seconds. Beat on high for 4 minutes. Coat a 10-in. fluted tube pan with nonstick cooking spray and dust with flour. Add batter. Bake at 350° for 50–55 minutes or until a toothpick inserted near the center comes out clean. Cool for 10 minutes before removing from pan to a wire rack to cool completely. Dust with confectioners' sugar. **Yield:** 16 servings.

Coconut Poppy Seed Cake

"This moist coconut cake is definitely one of my most requested desserts," says Gail Cayce of Wautoma, Wisconsin. *"For variety, you can use different cake mixes and pudding flavors."*

1 package (18¼ ounces) white cake mix
¼ cup poppy seeds
¼ teaspoon coconut extract, optional
3½ cups cold milk
2 packages (3.4 ounces *each*) instant coconut cream pudding mix
1 carton (8 ounces) frozen whipped topping, thawed
⅓ cup flaked coconut, toasted, optional

Prepare cake according to package directions, adding poppy seeds and coconut extract, if desired, to batter. Pour into a greased 13-in. × 9-in. × 2-in. baking pan. Bake at 350° for 20–25 minutes or until a toothpick inserted near the center comes out clean. Cool completely. In a mixing bowl, beat milk and pudding mix on low speed for 2 minutes. Spread over the cake. Spread with whipped topping. Sprinkle with coconut if desired. **Yield:** 20–24 servings.

Banana Fudge Cake

You'll love the banana flavor throughout this moist, fudgy cake and fluffy frosting from Jan Gregory of Bethel, Ohio. "This recipe was given to me by my mother-in-law. It's a favorite at family gatherings," Jan reports.

1 package (18¼ ounces) chocolate fudge cake mix
1 large ripe banana, mashed

FROSTING:
½ cup butter
¼ cup water
5½ cups confectioners' sugar, *divided*
¼ cup baking cocoa
1 small ripe banana, mashed
½ teaspoon vanilla extract

In a mixing bowl, prepare cake mix according to package directions, omitting ¼ cup of the water. Beat on low speed until moistened. Add banana; beat on high for 2 minutes. Pour into a greased 13-in. × 9-in. × 2-in. baking pan. Bake at 350° for 35–40 minutes or until a toothpick inserted near the center comes out clean. Cool completely. In a saucepan, heat butter and water until butter is melted; set aside. In a mixing bowl, combine 4 cups confectioners' sugar and cocoa. Add butter mixture, banana and vanilla; beat until smooth. Add enough remaining sugar until frosting reaches desired spreading consistency. Frost the cake. **Yield:** 12–15 servings.

Susie Sunshine Cake

This cake developed in the Taste of Home Test Kitchen is so light and lemony, folks will have a hard time believing it starts with a boxed mix. The frosting looks professional, but it's quite easy to blend. Fresh fruit provides the fun final touches.

1 package (9 ounces) yellow cake mix
1 carton (8 ounces) frozen whipped topping, thawed
1 teaspoon grated lemon peel
1 teaspoon grated orange peel
Red and yellow liquid food coloring
2 medium lemons, sliced and halved
2 medium oranges, sliced and halved
2 blueberries
1 large strawberry

Prepare and bake the cake according to package directions, using a greased and floured 8-in. round baking pan. Cool for 10 minutes; remove from pan to a wire rack to cool completely. Transfer to a 12- to 14-in. serving plate. Combine whipped topping and lemon and orange peels. Frost top and sides of cake. Place drops of red and yellow food coloring randomly over frosting. With a spatula, blend colors randomly. Alternate lemon and orange slices around base of cake to form rays. Add two orange slices and blueberries for eyes. Slice the strawberry; use two center slices for the mouth, placing them on the cake with straight edges touching. Refrigerate until serving. **Yield:** 6 servings.

Pineapple Layer Cake

"I often prepare this moist golden cake at Easter, but it's wonderful just about any time of year," relates Linda Sakal of Biloxi, Mississippi. Pineapple frosting provides the fast finishing touch.

1 package (18¼ ounces) yellow cake mix
1 can (11 ounces) mandarin oranges, drained
1 can (20 ounces) unsweetened crushed pineapple, drained
1 package (3.4 ounces) instant vanilla pudding mix
1 carton (12 ounces) frozen whipped topping, thawed

Prepare cake batter according to package directions. Beat in oranges until blended. Pour into two greased and floured 9-in. round baking pans. Bake at 350° for 25–30 minutes or until a toothpick inserted near the center comes out clean. Cool for 10 minutes before removing from pans to wire racks to cool completely. Combine pineapple and pudding mix; fold in whipped topping. Spread between layers and over top and sides of cake. Store in the refrigerator. **Yield:** 12 servings.

Chocolate Chip Snack Cake

"Instant pudding mix and cake mix cut the preparation time for this delicious cake that is loaded with grated chocolate and miniature chocolate chips," notes Karen Walker of Sterling, Virginia. "I often make it for weekend guests and work luncheons. It always goes over well."

1 package (18¼ ounces) yellow cake mix
1 package (3.4 ounces) instant vanilla pudding mix
4 eggs
1 cup water
½ cup vegetable oil
1 package (12 ounces) miniature semisweet chocolate chips
1 package (4 ounces) German sweet chocolate, grated, *divided*
Confectioners' sugar

In a mixing bowl, combine the first five ingredients; beat for 5 minutes. Stir in chocolate chips and half of the grated chocolate. Pour into a greased 13-in. × 9-in. × 2-in. baking pan. Bake at 350° for 45–50 minutes or until a toothpick inserted near the center comes out clean. Sprinkle with remaining grated chocolate while slightly warm. Cool completely. Dust with confectioners' sugar. **Yield:** 12–15 servings.

Raisin Pound Cake

Yellow cake mix, applesauce and raisins make this moist, pleasantly spiced loaf a no-fuss favorite of LuEllen Spaulding. "I turn to this recipe when unexpected guests drop by because I usually have the ingredients in the cupboard," notes the Caro, Michigan baker. For a special occasion, top slices with fresh fruit.

1 package (18¼ ounces) yellow cake mix
1 cup applesauce
½ cup water
¼ cup vegetable oil
3 eggs
½ teaspoon ground cinnamon
¼ teaspoon ground nutmeg
¼ teaspoon ground allspice
½ cup raisins

In a mixing bowl, combine cake mix, applesauce, water, oil, eggs, cinnamon, nutmeg and allspice. Beat on medium speed for 2 minutes. Stir in raisins. Pour into two greased 8-in. × 4-in. × 2-in. loaf pans. Bake at 350° for 45–50 minutes or until a toothpick inserted near the center comes out clean. Cool for 5–10 minutes before removing from pans to wire racks. **Yield:** 2 loaves.

Peanut Butter Brownies

"I came up with these fudgy peanut butter brownies when I ran out of ingredients I needed for my usual recipe," relates Marcella Cremer of Decatur, Illinois. "They take less than 10 minutes to mix up."

1 package (17½ ounces) peanut butter cookie mix
½ cup baking cocoa
⅔ cup chocolate syrup
¼ cup butter, melted
1 egg
½ cup chopped walnuts *or* peanuts

FROSTING
2 cups plus 2 tablespoons confectioners' sugar
½ cup chocolate syrup
¼ cup baking cocoa
¼ cup butter, melted
½ teaspoon vanilla extract

In a mixing bowl, combine cookie mix and cocoa. Add chocolate syrup, butter and egg; beat until combined. Stir in nuts. Spread into a greased 13-in. × 9-in. × 2-in. baking pan. Bake at 350° for 28–32 minutes or until a toothpick inserted near the center comes out clean. Cool on a wire rack. Meanwhile, combine the frosting ingredients in a bowl; stir until smooth. Spread over brownies. Cut into squares. **Yield:** 2 dozen. **Editor's Note:** This recipe was tested with Betty Crocker peanut butter cookie mix.

Citrus Mini Cakes

These moist, bite-size muffins from Linda Terrell of Palatka, Florida are melt-in-your-mouth good. "With their appealing look, they really dress up a party table," she notes. The recipe makes a big batch, so there's plenty to please a crowd.

1 package (18¼ ounces) **yellow cake mix**
1¼ cups **water**
3 **eggs**
⅓ cup **vegetable oil**
3½ cups **confectioners' sugar**
½ cup **orange juice**
¼ cup **lemon juice**
Toasted chopped almonds

In a mixing bowl, combine cake mix, water, eggs and oil; beat on low speed for 30 seconds. Beat on medium for 2 minutes. Fill well-greased miniature muffin cups two-thirds full. Bake at 350° for 10–12 minutes or until a toothpick inserted near the center comes out clean. Meanwhile, in a bowl, combine sugar and juices until smooth. Cool cakes for 2 minutes; remove from pans. Immediately dip cakes into glaze, coating well. Place top down on wire racks; sprinkle with almonds. **Yield:** about 6 dozen.

Strawberry Jam Bars

"I bake for a group of seniors every week," informs Karen Mead of Pittsburgh, Pennsylvania, *"and this is one of the goodies they request most. I always keep the ingredients on hand for last-minute baking emergencies."*

½ cup butter, softened
½ cup packed brown sugar
1 egg
1 package (18¼ ounces) white cake mix
1 cup finely crushed cornflakes
1 cup strawberry jam or preserves

In a mixing bowl, cream butter and brown sugar until smooth. Add egg; mix well. Gradually add cake mix and cornflakes. Set aside 1½ cups for topping. Press remaining dough into a greased 13-in. × 9-in. × 2-in. baking pan. Carefully spread jam over crust. Sprinkle with reserved dough; gently press down. Bake at 350° for 30 minutes or until golden brown. Cool completely on a wire rack. Cut into bars. **Yield:** 2 dozen.

Hugs 'n' Kisses Brownie

"When I needed a dessert in a hurry, I dressed up a brownie mix with on-hand ingredients to come up with this impressive treat," says Kristi Van Batavia of Kansas City, Missouri.

1 package fudge brownie mix (8-inch square pan size)
1 egg
¼ cup vegetable oil
¼ cup water
1½ cups vanilla *or* white chips, *divided*
14–16 milk chocolate kisses
14–16 striped chocolate kisses
1½ teaspoons shortening

In a bowl, stir brownie mix, egg, oil and water until well blended. Fold in 1 cup vanilla chips. Pour into a greased 9-in. heart-shaped or round springform pan. Bake at 350° for 35–40 minutes or until a toothpick inserted 2 in. from the side of pan comes out clean. Let stand for 10 minutes; alternate milk chocolate and striped kisses around edge of pan with points toward center. Melt shortening and remaining chips; stir until smooth. Drizzle over brownie. Cool completely. Remove sides of springform pan. **Yield:** 10-12 servings.

Brownie Delight

Brownie mix and instant pudding hurry along the preparation of this scrumptious layered dessert from Opal Erickson of Branson, Missouri. "My family asks for this rich treat for birthdays instead of a cake," she notes.

1 package brownie mix (13-inch × 9-inch pan size)
2 packages (one 8 ounces, one 3 ounces) cream cheese, softened
2 cups confectioners' sugar
1 carton (16 ounces) frozen whipped topping, thawed, divided
2 cups cold milk
1 package (3.9 ounces) instant chocolate pudding mix
½ cup chopped pecans

Prepare and bake brownies according to package directions, using a greased 13-in. × 9-in. × 2-in. baking pan. Cool completely. In a mixing bowl, beat cream cheese and sugar for 2 minutes. Fold in 2 cups whipped topping. Spread over brownies. In another bowl, combine the milk and pudding mix; beat until smooth. Refrigerate for 5 minutes; spread over the cream cheese layer. Spread with remaining whipped topping; sprinkle with pecans. Refrigerate until serving. **Yield:** 12–15 servings.

Malted Milk Cookies

"My daughter substituted crushed malted milk balls in our favorite chocolate chip cookie recipe to create these crisp treats," explains Audrey Metzger from Larchwood, Iowa. "They're so yummy fresh from the oven."

1 cup butter, softened
¾ cup packed brown sugar
⅓ cup sugar
1 egg
2 teaspoons vanilla extract
2¼ cups all-purpose flour
2 tablespoons instant chocolate drink mix
1 teaspoon baking soda
½ teaspoon salt
2 cups malted milk balls, crushed

In a mixing bowl, cream the butter and sugars. Beat in egg and vanilla. Combine the flour, drink mix, baking soda and salt; gradually add to creamed mixture. Stir in malted milk balls. Shape into 1½-in. balls. Place 2 in. apart on greased baking sheets. Bake at 375° for 10–12 minutes or until set. Cool for 1 minute before removing from pans to wire racks. **Yield:** about 3 dozen.

S'Mores Bars

Glowing campfire coals are not needed to enjoy the traditional taste of s'mores with this recipe from Kristine Brown of Rio Rancho, New Mexico. The tasty take-along treat makes a sweet snack any time of day.

8–10 **whole graham crackers**
   (about 5 inches × 2½ inches *each*)
1 **package fudge brownie mix**
   (13-inch × 9-inch pan size)
2 **cups miniature marshmallows**
1 **cup (6 ounces) semisweet chocolate chips**
⅔ **cup chopped peanuts**

Arrange graham crackers in a single layer in a greased 13-in. × 9-in. × 2-in. baking pan. Prepare the brownie batter according to package directions. Spread over crackers. Bake

at 350° for 25–30 minutes or until a toothpick inserted near the center comes out clean. Sprinkle with marshmallows, chocolate chips and peanuts. Bake 5 minutes longer or until marshmallows are slightly puffed and golden brown. Cool on a wire rack before cutting. **Yield:** 2 dozen.

Cinnamon Nut Cake

"This moist bundt cake is an easy-to-assemble treat for dessert or brunch," assures Margaret Wilson of Hemet, California. "Top with a dollop of whipped cream and you're ready to enjoy."

1 **package (18¼ ounces) yellow cake mix**
3 **eggs**
1⅓ **cups water**
¼ **cup vegetable oil**
1¼ **cups finely chopped walnuts**
7½ **teaspoons sugar**
4½ **teaspoons ground cinnamon**

In a mixing bowl, combine the cake mix, eggs, water and oil. Beat on medium speed for 2 minutes. Combine walnuts, sugar and cinnamon. Sprinkle a third of the nut mixture into a greased 10-in. fluted tube pan. Top with half of the batter and another third of the nut mixture. Repeat layers. Bake at 350° for 35–40 minutes or until a toothpick inserted near the center comes out clean. Cool for 10 minutes before removing from pan to a wire rack to cool completely. **Yield:** 12–14 servings.

Caramel-Fudge Chocolate Cake

"To satisfy the chocolate lovers in our family, I added hot fudge topping and chocolate chips to a caramel-covered dessert that's quite popular in our area," says Karen Stucky of Freeman, South Dakota. *"The moist cake layer is a breeze to prepare using a boxed mix…and the rich toppings make it especially decadent."*

1 package (18¼ ounces) chocolate cake mix
1 cup miniature semisweet chocolate chips, *divided*
1 jar (12¼ ounces) caramel ice cream topping, warmed
1 jar (11¾ ounces) hot fudge ice cream topping, warmed
1 carton (8 ounces) frozen whipped topping, thawed
½ cup English toffee bits *or* almond brickle chips

Prepare cake batter according to package directions. Stir in ¾ cup chocolate chips. Pour into a greased 13-in. × 9-in. × 2-in. baking pan. Bake at 350° for 35–40 minutes or until a toothpick inserted near the center comes out clean. Immediately poke holes in the cake with a meat fork or skewer. Spread caramel and fudge toppings over cake. Cool on a wire rack. Frost with whipped topping. Sprinkle with toffee bits and remaining chocolate chips. Store in the refrigerator. **Yield:** 12–15 servings.

Pumpkin Bundt Cake

"Our family grows lots of pumpkins, but I have to put dibs on some or the children will carve every one!" exclaims Margaret Slocum of Ridgefield, Washington. *"I like to use them in this moist cake."*

¼ cup butter, softened
1 cup sugar
1 cup packed brown sugar
4 eggs
1 can (15 ounces) solid-pack pumpkin
3 cups biscuit/baking mix

GLAZE:
1 cup confectioners' sugar
1 tablespoon milk
½ teaspoon vanilla extract

In a mixing bowl, cream butter and sugars. Add the eggs, one at a time, beating well after each. Beat in pumpkin; mix well. Gradually add baking mix until combined. Pour into a greased and floured 10-in. fluted tube pan. Bake at 350° for 55–60 minutes or until a toothpick inserted near the center comes out clean. Cool for 10 minutes before removing from pan to a wire rack. Combine glaze ingredients; drizzle over cooled cake. **Yield:** 12–16 servings.

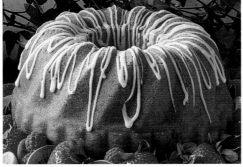

Root Beer Float Cake

Kat Thompson of Prineville, Oregon adds root beer to both the cake batter and fluffy frosting of this summery dessert to get that great root beer float taste. "Serve this moist cake to a bunch of hungry kids and watch it disappear," she advises.

1 package (18¼ ounces) white cake mix
1¾ cups cold root beer, *divided*
¼ cup vegetable oil
2 eggs
1 envelope whipped topping mix

In a mixing bowl, combine cake mix, 1¼ cups root beer, oil and eggs. Beat on low speed for 2 minutes or stir by hand for 3 minutes. Pour into a greased 13-in. × 9-in. × 2-in. baking pan. Bake at 350° for 30–35 minutes or until a toothpick inserted near the center comes out clean. Cool completely on a wire rack. In a mixing bowl, combine the whipped topping mix and remaining root beer. Beat until soft peaks form. Frost cake. Store in the refrigerator. **Yield:** 12–16 servings.

Dipped Peanut Butter Cookies

"Baking mix makes these soft, moist cookies a snap to stir up, yet they're pretty enough for parties," says Stephanie DeLoach of Magnolia, Arkansas. "I'm often asked to bring them to wedding and baby showers."

1 cup peanut butter
1 can (14 ounces) sweetened condensed milk
1 egg
1 teaspoon vanilla extract
2 cups biscuit/baking mix
¾–1 pound milk chocolate candy coating
1 tablespoon shortening

In a mixing bowl, combine peanut butter, milk, egg and vanilla; beat until smooth. Stir in biscuit mix; mix well. Cover and refrigerate for 1 hour. Shape into 1-in. balls and place 1 in. apart on ungreased baking sheets. Flatten each ball with the bottom of a glass. Bake at 350° for 8–10 minutes or until golden brown. Cool on wire racks. In a small saucepan over low heat, melt confectionery coating and shortening. Dip each cookie halfway into chocolate; shake off excess. Place on waxed paper-lined baking sheets to harden. **Yield:** about 5 dozen.

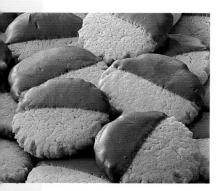

Carrot-Topped Cupcakes

The Taste of Home Test Kitchen dressed up a handy spice cake mix with shredded carrots and chopped walnuts for a delicious treat. The mini carrots are eye-catching, too.

1 package (18¼ ounces) spice cake mix
1½ cups shredded carrots
½ cup chopped walnuts
1 teaspoon ground cinnamon
1 can (16 ounces) cream cheese frosting
Orange paste food coloring
Fresh parsley sprigs

Prepare cake batter according to package directions. Fold in carrots, walnuts and cinnamon. Fill paper-lined muffin cups half full. Bake at 350° for 18–23 minutes or until a toothpick comes out clean. Remove from pans to wire racks to cool completely. Frost cupcakes with 1¼ cups frosting.

Place remaining frosting in a small resealable plastic bag; tint with orange food coloring. Cut a small hole in the corner of bag; pipe a carrot on the top of each cupcake. Add a parsley sprig for greens. **Yield:** 2 dozen.

Oatmeal Brownies

"This recipe makes the most of a handy packaged brownie mix, so they're fast to fix." notes Jennifer Trenhaile of Emerson, Nebraska. *"If you don't have the mini M&Ms, use chocolate chips instead. Our kids love these rich fudgy squares with a scoop of ice cream."*

1½ cups quick-cooking oats
1 cup M&M miniature baking bits
½ cup all-purpose flour
½ cup packed brown sugar
½ chopped walnuts
½ teaspoon baking soda
½ cup butter, melted
1 package fudge brownie mix
(13-inch × 9-inch pan size)

In a bowl, combine the first seven ingredients; mix well. Set aside 1 cup for topping. Pat the remaining mixture into a greased 15-in. × 10-in. × 1-in. baking pan. Prepare brownie batter according to package directions. Spread over the crust. Sprinkle with the reserved oat mixture. Bake at 350° for 25–30 minutes or until a toothpick inserted near the center comes out clean. Cool on a wire rack. Cut into bars. **Yield:** 5 dozen.

Chocolate Raspberry Bars

A boxed cake mix and raspberry jam simplify assembly of these sweet treats from Diana Olmstead. "The bars are very rich, so cut them into small pieces," suggests the Yelm, Washington cook.

1 package (18¼ ounces) devil's food cake mix
1 egg
⅓ cup butter, softened
1 jar (12 ounces) seedless raspberry jam

TOPPING:
1 package (10 to 12 ounces) vanilla *or* white chips
1 package (8 ounces) cream cheese, softened
2 tablespoons milk
½ cup semisweet chocolate chips
2 tablespoons butter

In a bowl, combine cake mix, egg and butter until crumbly. Press into a greased 15-in. × 10-in. × 1-in. baking pan. Bake at 350° for 8–10 minutes or until a toothpick inserted near the center comes out clean (crust will appear puffy and dry). Cool on a wire rack. Spread jam over the crust. In a microwave or heavy saucepan, melt vanilla chips; stir until smooth. In a mixing bowl, beat cream cheese and milk until smooth. Add melted chips; mix well. Carefully spread over jam. Melt chocolate chips and butter; stir until smooth. Drizzle or pipe over the cream cheese layer. Refrigerate before cutting. **Yield:** about 6 dozen.

Chocolate Chip Cake Bars

"Whenever I need a quick dessert for a bake sale or get-together, I rely on this recipe," notes Tammy Haugen of Mayville, Wisconsin. *"I keep cake mixes on hand, so these chocolate chip-studded treats are a snap to stir up."*

1 package (18¼ ounces) yellow cake mix
2 eggs
¼ cup packed brown sugar
¼ cup butter, melted
¼ cup water
2 cups (12 ounces) semisweet chocolate chips, *divided*
½ cup chopped pecans *or* walnuts
1 tablespoon shortening

In a mixing bowl, combine the first five ingredients. Beat on medium speed for 2 minutes. Stir in 1½ cups of chocolate chips and nuts. Spread in a greased 13-in. × 9-in. × 2-in. baking pan. Bake at 375° for 20–25 minutes or until lightly browned and a toothpick inserted near the center comes out clean. Cool on a wire rack. Melt shortening with the remaining chocolate chips; drizzle over the top. Cut into bars. **Yield:** about 3½ dozen.

CHAPTER 8

More
Sweet Treats

Quick Coconut Cream Pie

"I've found a way to make coconut cream pie without a lot of fuss and still get terrific flavor," notes Betty Claycomb of Alverton, Pennsylvania. *"Using a convenient purchased crust, instant pudding and frozen whipped topping, I can enjoy an old-time dessert even when time is short."*

   1 package (5.1 ounces) instant vanilla pudding mix
1½ cups cold milk
   1 carton (8 ounces) frozen whipped topping, thawed, *divided*
¾–1 cup flaked coconut, toasted, *divided*
   1 pastry shell, baked *or* graham cracker crust (8 *or* 9 inches)

In a mixing bowl, beat pudding and milk on low speed for 2 minutes. Fold in half of the whipped topping and ½ to ¾ cup of coconut. Pour into crust. Spread with remaining whipped topping; sprinkle with remaining coconut. Chill. **Yield:** 6–8 servings.

Cookies 'n' Cream Pie

"This creamy make-ahead dessert is perfect for company," remarks Julie Sterchi of Flora, Illinois. *Convenience foods—including instant pudding, frozen whipped topping, cookies and prepared crumb crust—make it a treat for the cook, too.*

1½ cups half-and-half cream
   1 package (3.4 ounces) instant vanilla pudding mix
   1 carton (8 ounces) frozen whipped topping, thawed
   1 cup crushed cream-filled chocolate sandwich cookies (about 11 cookies)
   1 chocolate crumb crust (9 inches)

In a mixing bowl, combine the cream and pudding mix; beat on medium speed for 1 minute. Let stand for 5 minutes. Fold in whipped topping and cookies. Spoon into crust. Freeze until firm, about 6 hours or overnight. May be frozen for up to 3 months. Remove from the freezer 10 minutes before serving. **Yield:** 6–8 servings.

Cranberry Brownie Torte

Canned cranberry sauce adds a festive finishing touch to this dessert from Gloria Kirchman of Eden Prairie, Minnesota. Folks are sure to find it irresistible.

1 package fudge brownie mix
(13-inch × 9-inch pan size)
2 eggs
½ cup vegetable oil
¼ cup water
½ cup chopped pecans

FILLING:
1 package (8 ounces) cream cheese, softened
½ cup cranberry juice
2 tablespoons sugar
1 carton (12 ounces) frozen whipped topping, thawed

TOPPING:
1 can (16 ounces) whole-berry cranberry sauce
Pecan halves, optional

In a bowl, combine brownie mix, eggs, oil and water; beat until combined. Fold in pecans. Transfer to a greased 10-in. springform pan. Bake at 350° for 35–40 minutes or until a toothpick inserted near the center comes out with moist crumbs. Cool completely. For filling, in a mixing bowl, beat the cream cheese, cranberry juice and sugar until smooth. Set aside 1 cup whipped topping for garnish. Fold remaining topping into cream cheese mixture. Carefully spread over brownie. Stir cranberry sauce; carefully spread over the filling. Garnish with reserved whipped topping and pecan halves if desired. Refrigerate for at least 2 hours before serving. Store leftovers in the refrigerator. **Yield:** 12 servings.

Strawberry Lemon Trifle

"This refreshingly fruity dessert is one of our favorites," notes Lynn Marie Frucci of Pullman, Washington. *"It looks so beautiful layered in a glass bowl that people will think you fussed. The secret is starting with a purchased angel food cake."*

4 ounces fat-free cream cheese, softened
1 cup fat-free lemon yogurt
2 cups fat-free milk
1 package (3.4 ounces) instant lemon pudding mix
2 teaspoons grated lemon peel
2½ cups sliced fresh strawberries, *divided*
1 tablespoon white grape juice *or* water
1 prepared angel food cake (10 inches)

In a mixing bowl, beat cream cheese and yogurt. Add the milk, pudding mix and lemon peel; beat until smooth. In a blender, process ½ cup strawberries and grape juice until smooth. Tear cake into 1-in. cubes; place a third in a trifle bowl or 3-qt. serving bowl. Top with a third of the pudding mixture and half of the remaining strawberries. Drizzle with half of the strawberry sauce. Repeat. Top with remaining cake and pudding mixture. Cover and refrigerate for at least 2 hours. **Yield:** 14 servings.

Easy Black Forest Torte

"This torte recipe is so easy," notes Deb Morrison of Skiatook, Oklahoma. *"All you need is four ingredients. The marshmallows and cherries trade places during baking—and the flavor is excellent!"*

5 cups miniature marshmallows
1 package (18¼ ounces) chocolate cake mix
1 can (21 ounces) cherry pie filling
1 carton (8 ounces) frozen whipped topping, thawed

Sprinkle marshmallows in a greased 13-in. × 9-in. × 2-in. baking pan. Prepare cake batter according to package directions; pour over the marshmallows.

Spoon pie filling over batter. Bake at 350° for 1 hour or until a toothpick inserted near the center comes out clean. Cool. Frost with whipped topping. Store in the refrigerator. **Yield:** 12–16 servings.

Pistachio Cookie Dessert

"With its smooth pistachio filling, this cool treat is a favorite refreshment at summer 4-H meetings," remarks Audrey Phillips of Gambier, Ohio. *"It's best made and frozen a day in advance,"* she recommends. *"It will thaw as you head to a picnic or potluck."*

1 quart vanilla ice cream
1 package (20 ounces) chocolate cream-filled sandwich cookies
½ cup plus 2 tablespoons butter, melted
1½ cups cold milk
2 packages (3.4 ounces *each*) instant pistachio pudding mix
1 carton (16 ounces) frozen whipped topping, thawed

Soften ice cream while preparing crust. Place cookies in a food processor or blender; cover and process until fine crumbs form. Stir in butter. Set aside 1 cup for topping. Press remaining crumb mixture into an ungreased 13-in. × 9-in. × 2-in. dish. In a mixing bowl, beat milk and pudding mix on low speed for 2 minutes. Gradually add ice cream; mix well. Fold in whipped topping. Spread over crust. Sprinkle reserved crumb mixture over top, pressing down lightly. Cover and freeze for 4 hours or overnight. Remove from the freezer 20 minutes before cutting. **Yield:** 12–15 servings.

Brownie Caramel Parfaits

Chris Schnittka of Charlottesville, Virginia easily transforms brownies, ice cream and caramel topping into a tempting treat. "Layers of toasted coconut and nuts add nice crunch and make this dessert seem fancy," she remarks, "but it really couldn't be simpler to put together."

½ cup chopped pecans
½ cup shredded coconut
1 package brownie mix (8-inch × 8-inch pan size)
1 pint vanilla ice cream
1 jar (12¼ ounces) caramel ice cream topping

Place pecans and coconut in an ungreased baking pan. Bake at 350° for 10–12 minutes or until toasted, stirring frequently. Meanwhile, prepare brownies according to package directions. Cool; cut into small squares. When ready to serve, layer the brownies, ice cream, caramel topping and pecan mixture in parfait or dessert glasses; repeat layers one or two times. **Yield:** 6 servings.
Editor's Note: Any type of nuts, ice cream or topping may be used in these parfaits.

Blackberry Breeze Pie

Gail Toepfer knows that making dessert doesn't necessarily require heating up her Iron Ridge, Wisconsin kitchen. "This fluffy no-bake treat is simple to fix with gelatin, whipped topping and fresh berries," she remarks. "Or try it with peaches or mandarin oranges and coordinating gelatin flavors."

1 package (3 ounces) black cherry *or* cherry gelatin
1 cup boiling water
1 cup cold water
1½ cups fresh blackberries
1 carton (8 ounces) frozen whipped topping, thawed
1 graham cracker crust (8 to 10 inches)

In a bowl, dissolve gelatin in boiling water. Stir in cold water. Refrigerate for 1 hour or until thickened. Gently fold in blackberries and whipped topping. Pour into crust. Chill for 2 hours or until serving. **Yield:** 8 servings.

Chocolate Peanut Dream Pie

"I love the flavor of peanut butter cups, so I dreamed up this creamy, rich pie to serve to company," says Rosanne Marshall of Depew, New York. *"It's wonderfully simple to make and always gets rave reviews."*

1 package (3.4 ounces) cook-and-serve chocolate
    pudding mix
½ cup creamy peanut butter
1 cup whipped topping
1 graham cracker crust (9 inches)
Peanuts and additional whipped topping, optional

Prepare pudding according to package directions. Remove from the heat; whisk in peanut butter. Place pan in a bowl of ice water for 5 minutes, stirring occasionally. Fold in whipped topping. Pour into the crust. Cover and refrigerate for 1 hour or until set. Garnish with peanuts and whipped topping if desired. **Yield:** 6–8 servings.

Blueberry Delight

Christine Halandras of Meeker, Colorado presents a delicious blueberry trifle. "Prepared angel food cake makes this impressive dessert a breeze to assemble," she assures. "Plus, it can be put together ahead so there's no last-minute fuss."

1 package (8 ounces) cream cheese, softened
½ cup confectioners' sugar
1 can (14 ounces) sweetened condensed milk
1 package (3.4 ounces) instant vanilla pudding mix
1 carton (12 ounces) frozen whipped topping,
    thawed, *divided*
1 angel food cake (10 inches), cut into 1-inch cubes
1 quart fresh *or* frozen blueberries, thawed
Additional blueberries, optional

In a mixing bowl, beat cream cheese and confectioners' sugar. Add milk and pudding mix; mix well. Fold in 1½ cups of whipped topping. Place half of the cake cubes in a 3-qt. glass bowl. Layer with half of the berries and pudding mixture. Cover with remaining cake cubes. Layer with remaining berries and pudding mixture. Spread remaining whipped topping over top. Garnish with additional berries if desired. Store leftovers in the refrigerator. **Yield:** 12–14 servings.

Peach Pudding

"This light peach dessert is so fresh it tastes just like summertime," says Shelby Nicodemus of New Carlisle, Ohio. "It's a quick way to dress up instant vanilla pudding."

¼ cup peach gelatin powder
½ cup hot milk
1½ cups cold milk
1 package (3.4 ounces) instant vanilla pudding mix
Sliced fresh peaches and whipped topping, optional

In a bowl, dissolve gelatin in hot milk; set aside. Meanwhile, in a mixing bowl, beat cold milk and pudding mix on low speed for 2 minutes. Add gelatin mixture; mix well. Let stand for 5 minutes. Spoon into individual dishes. Garnish with peaches and whipped topping if desired. **Yield:** 4 servings.

Black Forest Mousse

"If you like chocolate and cherries, you'll love this smooth, light dessert," assures Deanna Richter of Elmore, Minnesota. Pantry staples such as instant pudding and canned pie filling make it quick to fix.

2 cups milk
1 package (3.9 ounces) instant chocolate pudding mix
1 can (21 ounces) cherry pie filling
2 cups whipped topping

In a bowl, beat the milk and pudding mix for 2 minutes or until smooth. Let stand until slightly thickened, about 2 minutes. Stir in pie filling. Gently fold in whipped topping. Spoon into individual dessert dishes; refrigerate until serving. **Yield:** 8 servings.

Banana Pudding Dessert

Edna Perry of Rice, Texas blends cream cheese, sweetened condensed milk and whipped topping into instant pudding, then layers this creamy concoction with vanilla wafers and sliced bananas. Served in a glass bowl, the results make for a fancy yet fuss-free dessert.

1 package (8 ounces) cream cheese, softened
1 can (14 ounces) sweetened condensed milk
1 cup cold milk
1 package (3.4 ounces) instant vanilla pudding mix
1 carton (8 ounces) frozen whipped topping, thawed
52 vanilla wafers
4 medium firm bananas, sliced

In a mixing bowl, beat cream cheese until smooth. Beat in condensed milk; set aside. In another bowl, whisk milk and pudding mix; add to cream cheese mixture. Fold in whipped topping. Place a third of the vanilla wafers in a 2½-qt. glass bowl. Top with a third of the bananas and pudding mixture. Repeat layers twice. Refrigerate until serving. **Yield:** 10–12 servings.

Vanilla Fruit Dessert

Julie Scott of Pratt, Kansas shares her quick and easy recipe. "A package of instant vanilla pudding mix is the starting point of this easy, creamy topping that dresses up fresh fruit," she says.

½ cup cold milk
1 package (3.4 ounces) instant vanilla pudding mix
1 cup (8 ounces) vanilla yogurt
½ cup orange juice concentrate
4–6 cups assorted fruit (apples, grapes, mandarin oranges, etc.)

In a mixing bowl, combine milk, pudding mix, yogurt and orange juice concentrate. Beat on low speed for 2 minutes. Serve over fruit. Refrigerate any leftover topping. **Yield:** 1¾ cups topping (4–6 servings).

Chocolate Praline Torte

"No one will know this fancy dessert started with a handy boxed cake mix," assures Sandra Castillo of Watertown, Wisconsin. "We enjoy the scrumptious treat throughout the year for special dinners, potlucks and even picnics."

1 cup packed brown sugar
½ cup butter
¼ cup heavy whipping cream
¾ cup coarsely chopped pecans
1 package (18¼ ounces) devil's food cake mix

TOPPING:
1¾ cups heavy whipping cream
¼ cup confectioners' sugar
¼ teaspoon vanilla extract
Chocolate curls, optional

In a saucepan, combine brown sugar, butter and cream. Stir over low heat until butter is melted. Pour into two greased 9-in. round cake pans. Sprinkle with pecans; set aside. Prepare cake mix according to package directions. Carefully pour batter over pecans. Bake at 325° for 35–45 minutes or until a toothpick comes out clean. Cool in pans for 10 minutes; invert onto wire racks to cool completely. For topping, beat cream in a mixing bowl until soft peaks form. Add sugar and vanilla; beat until stiff. Place one cake layer, pecan side up, on a serving plate. Spread with half of the topping. Top with second cake layer and remaining topping. Garnish with chocolate curls if desired. Store in the refrigerator. **Yield:** 8–10 servings.

Easy Cocoa Mousse

"This airy, melt-in-your-mouth mousse has a light cocoa flavor that's so good," comments Donna Brooks of Jefferson, Maine. "It's simple to mix, then pop in the fridge while you're preparing the rest of your meal."

  1 **envelope unflavored gelatin**
  ¼ **cup cold water**
1¼ **cups fat-free milk**
Artificial sweetener equivalent to ⅓ cup sugar
  ¼ **cup baking cocoa**
  1 **teaspoon vanilla extract**
1¾ **cups reduced-fat whipped topping,** *divided*

In a small saucepan, sprinkle gelatin over water; let stand for 5 minutes. Cook over low heat until gelatin is dissolved. In a blender or food processor, combine milk, sweetener, cocoa and vanilla. Slowly add gelatin mixture. Fold in 1½ cups whipped topping. Spoon into serving dishes. Cover and chill for at least 1 hour. Garnish with remaining topping. **Yield:** 6 servings.

Chocolate Berry Parfaits

"This creamy dessert is easy to make for weekday dinners, yet pretty enough for company," assures Lynn McAllister of Mount Ulla, North Carolina. "For quicker results, use whipped topping rather than whipping cream…or serve in a single bowl."

  2 **cups cold milk**
  1 **package (3.9 ounces) instant chocolate pudding mix**
  1 **package (10 ounces) frozen sweetened strawberries, thawed**
  1 **cup heavy whipping cream**
  ¼ **cup confectioners' sugar**
Sliced fresh strawberries, optional

In a mixing bowl, beat milk and pudding mix until thick and smooth, about 2 minutes; set aside. Drain strawberries (discard the juice or save for another use); place berries in a blender. Cover and process until smooth; set aside. In a mixing bowl, beat cream and sugar until stiff peaks form. Gently fold in strawberry puree. Divide half of the chocolate pudding among four or six parfait glasses or bowls. Top with half of the strawberry mixture. Repeat layers. Garnish with a strawberry slice if desired. **Yield:** 4–6 servings.
Editor's Note: 2 cups of whipped topping may be substituted for the whipping cream and sugar.

Cappuccino Pudding

"With its fun combination of chocolate, coffee and cinnamon, this smooth dessert is one of my favorites," says Cindy Bertrand of Floydada, Texas. A garnish of whipped topping and chocolate wafer crumbs provides additional appeal.

4 teaspoons instant coffee granules
1 tablespoon boiling water
1½ cups cold fat-free milk
1 package (1.4 ounces) instant sugar-free chocolate pudding mix
½ teaspoon ground cinnamon
1 cup reduced-fat whipped topping
Additional whipped topping and chocolate wafer crumbs, optional

Dissolve coffee in water; set aside. In a mixing bowl, combine milk, pudding mix and cinnamon. Beat on low speed for 2 minutes. Stir in coffee. Fold in whipped topping. Spoon into serving dishes. Garnish with whipped topping and wafer crumbs if desired. **Yield:** 4 servings.

Kool-Aid Sherbet

"The recipe for this frosty treat is more than 30 years old, and kids love it," reports Elizabeth Stanton of Mt. Vernon, Washington. Powdered soft drink mix provides the yummy flavor.

1 cup sugar
1 envelope unsweetened orange Kool-Aid *or* flavor of your choice
3 cups milk

In a bowl, stir sugar, Kool-Aid mix and milk until sugar is dissolved. Pour into a shallow freezer container; cover and freeze for 1 hour or until slightly thickened. Transfer to a mixing bowl; beat until smooth. Return to freezer container; cover and freeze until firm. Remove from the freezer 20 minutes before serving. **Yield:** about 3 cups.

Melon Mousse

"This unique summer dessert is low in fat and a creative way to use cantaloupe," says Sandy McKenzie from Braham, Minnesota. "It's best when made with very ripe melon to give the sweetest flavor."

2 envelopes unflavored gelatin
3 tablespoons lemon juice
4 cups cubed ripe cantaloupe
1 tablespoon sugar
1 carton (8 ounces) fat-free lemon yogurt
Fresh raspberries, optional

In a small saucepan, sprinkle gelatin over lemon juice; let stand for 1 minute. Cook over low heat until gelatin is dissolved. Place cantaloupe, sugar and gelatin mixture in a blender; cover and process until smooth. Transfer to a bowl; stir in yogurt. Spoon into individual dishes; chill until firm. Garnish with raspberries if desired. **Yield:** 6 servings.

Festive Fruit Pie

Fresh banana slices, canned pineapple tidbits and chopped pecans dress up the cherry filling in this fuss-free pie from Dorothy Smith of El Dorado, Arkansas. For quicker results, you can substitute a prepared graham cracker crust for the baked pastry shell.

1 cup sugar
¼ cup all-purpose flour
1 can (21 ounces) cherry pie filling
1 can (14 ounces) pineapple tidbits, drained
1 package (3 ounces) orange gelatin
3–4 medium firm bananas, sliced
1 cup chopped pecans
2 pastry shells, baked (9 inches)
Whipped topping, optional

In a saucepan, combine sugar and flour. Stir in pie filling and pineapple. Bring to a boil over medium heat; cook and stir for 2 minutes or until thickened. Remove from the heat; stir in gelatin. Cool. Stir in the bananas and pecans. Pour into pie shells. Refrigerate for 3 hours. Garnish with whipped topping if desired. **Yield:** 2 pies (6–8 servings each).

Great Pumpkin Dessert

In Fountain Valley, California, Linda Guyot relies on canned pumpkin and a yellow cake mix to fix this alternative to pumpkin pie. "It's a tried-and-true dessert that always elicits compliments," she says.

1 can (15 ounces) solid-pack pumpkin
1 can (12 ounces) evaporated milk
3 eggs
1 cup sugar
4 teaspoons pumpkin pie spice
1 package (18¼ ounces) yellow cake mix
¾ cup butter, melted
1½ cups chopped walnuts
Vanilla ice cream *or* whipped cream

In a mixing bowl, combine the first five ingredients. Transfer to a greased 13-in. × 9-in. × 2-in. baking pan. Sprinkle with cake mix and drizzle with butter. Top with walnuts. Bake at 350° for 1 hour or until a knife inserted near the center comes out clean. Serve with ice cream or whipped cream. **Yield:** 12–16 servings.

Chocolate Dream Dessert

Kathleen Gordon makes a crowd-pleasing dessert simply with cake cubes, instant pudding, whipped topping, chocolate syrup and nuts. "It's a surefire way to satisfy chocolate lovers," remarks the Treadway, Tennessee cook.

1 package (18¼ ounces) chocolate cake mix
1 package (3.4 ounces) instant vanilla pudding mix
1 cup chocolate syrup, *divided*
1 carton (12 ounces) frozen whipped topping, thawed
½ cup chopped pecans

Prepare and bake the cake according to package directions, using a greased 13-in. × 9-in. × 2-in. baking pan. Cool on a wire rack. Meanwhile, prepare pudding according to package directions; pour into a 13-in. × 9-in. × 2-in. dish. Tear cake into small pieces and gently push down into the pudding. Drizzle with ¾ cup of chocolate syrup. Spread with whipped topping. Drizzle with remaining chocolate syrup. Sprinkle with pecans. Refrigerate until serving. **Yield:** 16–20 servings.

Brownie Swirl Cheesecake

"It may look fancy, but this cheesecake is so simple," assures Janet Brunner of Burlington, Kentucky. "The secret is the speedy crust— it's from a packaged brownie mix! You don't need to be an experienced cook to make the elegant chocolate swirls on top—anyone can do it."

1 package (8 ounces) brownie mix
2 packages (8 ounces *each*) cream cheese, softened
½ cup sugar
1 teaspoon vanilla extract
2 eggs
1 cup milk chocolate chips, melted
Whipped cream and miniature chocolate kisses, optional

Prepare brownie mix according to package directions for chewy fudge brownies. Spread into a greased 9-in. spring-form pan. Bake at 350° for 15 minutes (brownies will not test done). Cool for 10 minutes on a wire rack. Meanwhile, in a mixing bowl, combine cream cheese, sugar and vanilla; mix well. Add eggs, one at a time, beating well after each addition. Pour over the brownie crust. Top with melted chocolate; cut through batter with a knife to swirl the chocolate. Bake at 350° for 35–40 minutes or until center is almost set. Run a knife around edge of pan to loosen; cool completely. Remove sides of pan; refrigerate for at least 3 hours. Garnish with whipped cream and chocolate kisses if desired. **Yield:** 8–10 servings.

Tropical Fruit Cream Pie

Carolyn Dixon of Monticello, Arkansas uses crunchy toasted coconut to add a special touch to this sweet and fruity pie. It can be stirred up in a jiffy with handy pantry staples.

2 cups cold milk
1 package (3.4 ounces) instant coconut cream
   pudding mix
1 can (15¼ ounces) tropical fruit salad, drained
½ cup flaked coconut, toasted
1 graham cracker crust (9 inches)

In a bowl, beat milk and pudding mix for 2 minutes or until smooth. Let stand until slightly thickened, about 2 minutes. Add fruit and coconut; mix well. Pour into crust. Refrigerate until serving. **Yield:** 6–8 servings.

Banana Split Pudding

"Our kids love banana splits, so I came up with this simple dessert," explains Sherry Lee of Shelby, Alabama. "It's a hit with the entire family."

3 cups cold milk
1 package (5.1 ounces) instant vanilla pudding mix
1 medium firm banana, sliced
1 cup sliced fresh strawberries
1 can (8 ounces) crushed pineapple, drained
1 carton (8 ounces) frozen whipped topping, thawed
¼ cup chocolate syrup
¼ cup chopped pecans
Additional sliced strawberries and bananas, optional

In a bowl, whisk milk and pudding mix for 2 minutes. Add banana, strawberries and pineapple; transfer to a serving bowl. Dollop with whipped topping. Drizzle with chocolate syrup; sprinkle with pecans. Top with strawberries and bananas if desired. **Yield:** 6–8 servings.

Rocky Road Fudge Pops

"These sweet frozen treats are simple to prepare and guaranteed to bring out the kid in anyone," promises Karen Grant of Tulare, California. The creamy pops feature a special chocolate and peanut topping.*

1 package (3.4 ounces) cook-and-serve chocolate pudding mix
2½ cups milk
½ cup chopped peanuts
½ cup miniature semisweet chocolate chips
12 plastic cups (3 ounces *each*)
½ cup marshmallow creme
12 Popsicle sticks

In a large microwave-safe bowl, combine pudding mix and milk. Microwave, uncovered, on high for 6–7½ minutes or until bubbly and slightly thickened, stirring every 2 minutes. Cool for 20 minutes, stirring several times. Meanwhile, combine peanuts and chocolate chips; place about 2 tablespoons in each plastic cup. Stir marshmallow creme into pudding; spoon into cups. Insert Popsicle sticks; freeze. **Yield:** 12 servings. **Editor's Note:** This recipe was tested in an 850-watt microwave.

Peanut Butter Snack Cups

"When our kids were little, they loved this cool and creamy summertime treat," relates Nancy Clark of Cochranton, Pennsylvania. *"We'd keep several batches in the freezer so there were plenty when their neighborhood friends came over to play."*

12 vanilla wafers
1 carton (8 ounces) frozen whipped topping, thawed, *divided*
1 cup cold milk
½ cup peanut butter
1 package (3.9 ounces) instant chocolate pudding mix

Place wafers in paper- or foil-lined muffin cups. Top each with 1 tablespoon whipped topping. In a mixing bowl, combine milk and peanut butter. Add pudding mix; beat on low speed for 2 minutes. Fold in remaining whipped topping. Spoon into prepared cups. Cover and freeze. Remove from the freezer 10 minutes before serving. **Yield:** 12 servings.

Caramel Fudge Cheesecake

"It's hard to resist this chocolaty cheesecake with its fudgy crust, crunchy pecans and gooey layer of caramel," says Brenda Ruse of Truro, Nova Scotia. *"I combined several recipes to create this version that satisfies both the chocolate lovers and the cheesecake lovers in my family."*

1 package fudge brownie mix (8-inch square pan size)
1 package (14 ounces) caramels
¼ cup evaporated milk
1¼ cups coarsely chopped pecans
2 packages (8 ounces *each*) cream cheese, softened
½ cup sugar
2 eggs
2 squares (1 ounce *each*) semisweet chocolate, melted
2 squares (1 ounce *each*) unsweetened chocolate, melted

Prepare brownie batter according to the package directions. Spread into a greased 9-in. springform pan. Bake at 350° for 20 minutes. Cool for 10 minutes on a wire rack. Meanwhile, in a microwave-safe bowl, melt caramels with milk. Pour over brownie crust; sprinkle with pecans. In a mixing bowl, combine the cream cheese and sugar; mix well. Add eggs, beating on low speed just until combined. Stir in melted chocolate. Pour over pecans. Bake at 350° for 35–40 minutes or until the center is almost set. Cool on a wire rack for 10 minutes. Run a knife around edge of pan to loosen; cool completely. Chill overnight. Remove sides of pan before serving. Store leftovers in the refrigerator. **Yield:** 12 servings. **Editor's Note:** This recipe was tested using Hershey brand caramels.

S'More Tarts

Trish Quinn of Cheyenne, Wyoming brings a fireside favorite indoors with the taste-tempting treats she fixes for movie and game nights. Kids of all ages will quickly gobble up these individual graham cracker tarts filled with a fudgy brownie and golden marshmallows before asking, "Can I have s'more?"

1 package fudge brownie mix
  (13-inch × 9-inch pan size)
12 individual graham cracker shells
1½ cups miniature marshmallows
1 cup milk chocolate chips

Prepare brownie batter according to package directions. Place graham cracker shells on a baking sheet and fill with brownie batter. Bake at 350° for 20–25 minutes or until a toothpick inserted in the center comes out with moist crumbs. Immediately sprinkle with marshmallows and chocolate chips. Bake 3–5 minutes longer or until marshmallows are puffed and golden brown. **Yield:** 1 dozen.

Pineapple Fluff Pie

Jane Rhodes of Silverdale, Washington shares her recipe for a tasty pie. "This dessert has been a lifesaver for more than 20 years of entertaining and potlucks" she says.

1 can (20 ounces) unsweetened crushed pineapple,
  drained
1 package (3.4 ounces) instant lemon pudding mix
1 carton (8 ounces) frozen whipped topping, thawed
1 graham cracker crust (9 inches)

In a bowl, combine the pineapple and pudding mix until thickened; fold in the whipped topping. Spoon into crust. Refrigerate until serving. **Yield:** 8 servings.

Cookies 'n' Cream Fluff

"I created this recipe when I had spur-of-the-moment guests," recalls Renee Endress of Galva, Illinois. *"I needed something speedy and simple enough to make from ingredients I had in my pantry. It was an instant hit and is now a family favorite."*

2 cups cold milk
1 package (3.4 ounces) instant vanilla pudding mix
1 carton (8 ounces) frozen whipped topping, thawed
15 chocolate cream-filled sandwich cookies, broken into chunks
Additional broken cookies, optional

In a bowl, whisk milk and pudding mix for 2 minutes or until slightly thickened. Fold in whipped topping and cookies. Spoon into dessert dishes. Top with additional cookies if desired. Refrigerate until serving. **Yield:** 6 servings.

Lime Chiffon Dessert

"This make-ahead recipe was given to me by an aunt many years ago," notes Joyce Key of Snellville, Georgia. *"Her recipe called for lemon gelatin, but we like this dessert with more of a bite to it, so we use lime instead."*

1½ cups crushed graham crackers (about 24 squares)
⅓ cup sugar
½ cup butter, melted

FILLING:
1 package (3 ounces) lime gelatin
1 cup boiling water
2 packages (one 8 ounces, one 3 ounces) cream cheese, softened
1 cup sugar
1 teaspoon vanilla extract
1 carton (16 ounces) frozen whipped topping, thawed

Combine the first three ingredients; set aside 2 tablespoons for topping. Press remaining crumbs onto the bottom of an ungreased 13-in. × 9-in. × 2-in. baking dish; set aside. In a bowl, dissolve gelatin in boiling water; cool. In a mixing bowl, beat cream cheese and sugar. Add vanilla; mix well. Slowly add gelatin until combined. Fold in whipped topping. Spoon over crust; sprinkle with reserved crumbs. Cover and refrigerate for 3 hours or until set. **Yield:** 12–15 servings.

Chocolate Raspberry Dessert

Guests are sure to find wedges of this fruity frozen pie irresistible. The crustless concoction from Judy Schut of Grand Rapids, Michigan has a creamy mousse-like consistency that's melt-in-your-mouth good.

1 cup reduced-fat cottage cheese
¾ cup fat-free milk
⅓ cup raspberry spreadable fruit
1 package (1.4 ounces) instant sugar-free chocolate pudding mix
1 carton (8 ounces) reduced-fat frozen whipped topping, thawed
1 square (1 ounce) semisweet chocolate, melted
½ cup unsweetened raspberries

In a blender, combine cottage cheese, milk and spreadable fruit; cover and process until smooth. Add pudding mix and mix well. Pour into a bowl; fold in whipped topping. Spoon into a 9-in. pie plate. Drizzle with chocolate. Cover and freeze for 8 hours or overnight. Let stand at room temperature for 20 minutes before serving. Garnish with raspberries. **Yield:** 8 servings.

Almond Chocolate Torte

This no-bake chocolate dessert from Rhonda Lanterman of Terrace, British Columbia has a tasty almond crust and smooth fluffy filling that's almost like a mousse. "It's so simple to make ahead of time and so delicious," she says.

⅔ cup sliced almonds, toasted
8 squares (1 ounce *each*) semisweet chocolate
2 packages (8 ounces *each*) cream cheese, softened
1 cup sugar
1 envelope unflavored gelatin
¼ cup cold water
2 cups heavy whipping cream, whipped

Set aside 1 tablespoon almonds for garnish. Chop remaining almonds; sprinkle into a greased 9-in. springform pan. In a microwave or heavy saucepan, melt chocolate; stir until smooth. Cool slightly. In a mixing bowl, beat cream cheese and sugar. In a small saucepan, sprinkle gelatin over cold water; let stand for 1 minute. Cook and stir over low heat until gelatin is completely dissolved. Beat into cream cheese mixture. Add melted chocolate; beat until blended. Fold in the whipped cream. Pour into prepared pan. Sprinkle with reserved almonds. Cover and refrigerate for at least 3 hours. **Yield:** 10–12 servings.

Lime Yogurt Pie

A prepared crust makes this pie from Rhonda Olivieri of East Earl, Pennsylvania easy to whip up. "While the pie chills in the refrigerator, I prepare whatever main dish I'm serving for dinner," she notes.

1 package (3 ounces) lime gelatin
2 cartons (6 ounces *each*) key lime pie yogurt
1 carton (8 ounces) frozen whipped topping, thawed
1 graham cracker crust (9 inches)

In a bowl, combine gelatin powder and yogurt. Fold in whipped topping. Spread into crust. Refrigerate for at least 20 minutes before serving. **Yield:** 6–8 servings.

Butter Crunch Pudding

"A sweet crumb topping makes this simple pudding taste special," informs Kathy Giesbrecht of Prespatou, British Columbia. "Although our family prefers lemon, it's also good with other flavors of instant pudding."

1 cup all-purpose flour
½ cup flaked coconut
¼ cup packed brown sugar
½ cup cold butter
2 cups cold milk
1 package (3.4 ounces) instant lemon pudding mix *or* flavor of your choice

In a bowl, combine flour, coconut and brown sugar; cut in butter until crumbly. Spread the crumb mixture on a 15-in. × 10-in. × 1-in. baking pan. Bake at 375° for 15 minutes, stirring once. Cool slightly. Meanwhile, in a mixing bowl, beat milk and pudding mix for 1 minute or until slightly thickened; chill for 5 minutes. Spoon half of the crumbs into four dessert bowls. Top with pudding and remaining crumb mixture. **Yield:** 4 servings.

Chocolate and Fruit Trifle

"This refreshing dessert layered with devil's food cake, a creamy pudding mixture, red berries and green kiwi is perfect for the holidays or any special occasion," notes Angie Dierikx of State Center, Iowa. *"I like making it in a clear glass trifle bowl to show off its festive colors."*

1 package (18¼ ounces) devil's food cake mix
1 can (14 ounces) sweetened condensed milk
1 cup cold water
1 package (3.4 ounces) instant vanilla pudding mix
2 cups heavy whipping cream, whipped
2 tablespoons orange juice
2 cups fresh strawberries, chopped
2 cups fresh raspberries
2 kiwifruit, peeled and chopped

Prepare cake batter according to package directions; pour into a greased 15-in. × 10-in. × 1-in. baking pan. Bake at 350° for 20 minutes or until a toothpick inserted near the center comes out clean. Cool completely on a wire rack. Crumble enough cake to measure 8 cups; set aside. (Save remaining cake for another use.) In a mixing bowl, combine milk and water until smooth. Add pudding mix; beat on low speed for 2 minutes or until slightly thickened. Fold in the whipped cream. To assemble, spread 2½ cups pudding mixture in a 4-qt. glass bowl. Top with half of the crumbled cake; sprinkle with 1 tablespoon orange juice. Arrange half of the berries and kiwi over cake. Repeat pudding and cake layers; sprinkle with remaining orange juice. Top with remaining pudding mixture. Spoon remaining fruit around edge of bowl. Cover and refrigerate until serving. **Yield:** 12–16 servings.

Pineapple Ambrosia

In Adams, New York, Marguerite Widrick adds whipped topping to convenient pantry items to create this light and fluffy dessert. Toasted coconut and sweet pineapple give the creamy combination a tropical taste.

1 can (20 ounces) pineapple tidbits
1 package (3.4 ounces) instant coconut cream *or* vanilla pudding mix
1 carton (8 ounces) frozen whipped topping, thawed
4 tablespoons flaked coconut, toasted, *divided*
Maraschino cherries, optional
1 teaspoon maraschino cherry juice, optional

Drain pineapple, reserving juice; set pineapple aside. In a mixing bowl, combine pineapple juice and pudding mix; beat on low speed for 2 minutes or until thickened. Fold in whipped topping. Stir in pineapple and 3 tablespoons coconut. Transfer to a serving bowl. Garnish with remaining coconut, cherries and cherry juice if desired. Chill until serving. **Yield:** 6 servings.

Creamy Lemonade Pie

"This luscious lemon pie looks quite elegant for a special dinner, yet it requires little effort," notes Carolyn Griffin of Macon, Georgia. *"Guests will never suspect they're eating a quick-and-easy dessert."*

1 can (5 ounces) evaporated milk
1 package (3.4 ounces) instant lemon pudding mix
2 packages (8 ounces *each*) cream cheese, softened
¾ cup lemonade concentrate
1 graham cracker crust (9 inches)

In a mixing bowl, combine milk and pudding mix; beat on low speed for 2 minutes (mixture will be thick). In another mixing bowl, beat cream cheese until light and fluffy, about 3 minutes. Gradually beat in lemonade concentrate. Gradually beat in pudding mixture. Pour into crust. Cover and refrigerate for at least 4 hours. **Yield:** 6–8 servings.

Quick Fruitcake

"This moist loaf is the perfect choice for people who don't like the candied fruits that go into traditional fruitcake," assures Diane Hixon of Niceville, Florida. *"Each slice is chock-full of goodies, so they'll think that you fussed when you haven't."*

1 package (15.6 ounces) cranberry *or* blueberry quick bread mix
½ cup chopped pecans
½ cup raisins *or* chopped dates
¼ cup chopped maraschino cherries
¼ cup crushed pineapple, drained

Prepare quick bread batter according to package directions. Stir in the remaining ingredients. Pour into a greased 9-in. × 5-in. × 3-in. loaf pan. Bake at 350° for 55–60 minutes or until a toothpick inserted near the center comes out clean. Cool for 10 minutes before removing from pan to a wire rack. **Yield:** 1 loaf.

Orange Cream Dessert

For a light and refreshing ending to a meal, Peggy Detjen of Lakeville, Minnesota fills a cookie crumb crust with a combination of orange gelatin and ice cream. "You can use other flavors of gelatin," she shares. "I top slices with a dollop of whipped cream."

2 cups crushed cream-filled chocolate sandwich cookies (about 20 cookies)
⅓ cup butter *or* margarine, melted
1 package (6 ounces) orange *or* lime gelatin
2 cups boiling water
1 quart vanilla ice cream, softened

In a bowl, combine cookie crumbs and butter; set aside ¼ cup for topping. Press remaining crumb mixture into a greased 13-in. × 9-in. × 2-in. dish. In a bowl, dissolve gelatin in water; cover and refrigerate for 10 minutes. Stir in ice cream until smooth. Pour over the crust. Sprinkle with reserved crumb mixture. Chill until firm. **Yield:** 12–15 servings.

Gelatin Game Chips

It's a safe bet these gelatin gems from the Taste of Home Test Kitchen will delight a full house of friends.

½ cup milk
½ cup sugar
3 envelopes unflavored gelatin
¾ cup cold water
1½ teaspoons vanilla extract
2 cups (16 ounces) sour cream
5 cups lemon-lime soda
4 packages (3 ounces *each*) berry blue gelatin
4 packages (3 ounces *each*) raspberry gelatin

In a saucepan, heat milk and sugar over low heat until sugar is dissolved. Soften unflavored gelatin in water; stir into the milk mixture until dissolved. Remove from the heat; add vanilla. Cool to lukewarm; blend in sour cream. Pour into a 13-in. × 9-in. × 2-in. dish. Chill until set. In a saucepan, bring the soda to a boil. Place blue gelatin in a bowl; stir in 2½ cups of soda until gelatin is dissolved. Pour into another 13-in. × 9-in. × 2-in. dish. Repeat with raspberry gelatin and remaining soda. Refrigerate until set. Using a 1½-in. round cookie cutter, cut white, blue and red gelatin into rounds. Stack or scatter on a serving plate. **Yield:** 9 dozen.

Creamy Raspberry Pie

"The only thing difficult about my Creamy Raspberry Pie is letting it chill," notes Lorna Nault of Chesterton, Indiana. *"We can't wait for that first light, fluffy slice. It's especially pleasant during warm weather. Depending on what's in season, I might substitute blueberries or strawberries and complementary gelatin flavors."*

1 package (3 ounces) raspberry gelatin
½ cup boiling water
1 cup frozen vanilla yogurt
1 cup fresh *or* frozen unsweetened raspberries
¼ cup lime juice
2 cups whipped topping
1 graham cracker crust (9 inches)
Lime slices and additional raspberries and whipped
    topping, optional

In a bowl, dissolve gelatin in boiling water. Stir in frozen yogurt until melted. Add the raspberries and lime juice. Fold in whipped topping. Spoon into crust. Refrigerate for 3 hours or until firm. Garnish with lime, raspberries and whipped topping if desired. **Yield:** 8 servings.

Eclair Torte

"This is the perfect recipe for folks who like eclairs but don't have the time to make them," says Kathy Shepard of Shepherd, Michigan. *"This is a tried-and-true favorite for my family. My sons prefer this to a traditional birthday cake."*

1 cup water
½ cup butter
¼ teaspoon salt
1 cup all-purpose flour
4 eggs
1 package (8 ounces) cream cheese, softened
2 packages (3.4 ounces *each*) instant vanilla pudding mix
3 cups cold milk
1 carton (12 ounces) frozen whipped topping, thawed
Chocolate syrup

In a saucepan over medium heat, bring water, butter and salt to a boil. Add flour all at once; stir until a smooth ball forms. Remove from the heat; let stand for 5 minutes. Add eggs, one at a time, beating well with a wooden spoon after each addition. Beat until smooth. Spread into a greased 13-in. × 9-in. × 2-in. baking pan. Bake at 400° for 30–35 minutes or until puffed and golden brown. Cool completely on a wire rack. If desired, remove puff from pan and place on a serving platter. In a mixing bowl, beat cream cheese, pudding mix and milk until smooth. Spread over puff; refrigerate for 20 minutes. Spread with whipped topping; refrigerate. Drizzle with chocolate syrup just before serving. Refrigerate leftovers. **Yield:** 12 servings.

Peanut Butter Icebox Dessert

Leftover crushed cookies create the yummy crust for this crowd-pleasing dessert from Nancy Mueller of Bloomington, Minnesota. It's covered with a smooth cream cheese mixture, chocolate pudding and whipped topping for a lovely layered look.

2¼ cups crushed peanut butter cookies (about 11 cookies)
¼ cup sugar
¼ cup butter, melted
2 packages (3 ounces *each*) cream cheese, softened
1 cup confectioners' sugar
1 carton (8 ounces) frozen whipped topping, thawed, *divided*
2½ cups cold milk
2 packages (3.9 ounces *each*) instant chocolate pudding mix
Additional peanut butter cookies, broken into pieces

In a bowl, combine crushed cookies, sugar and butter; press into an ungreased 13-in. × 9-in. × 2-in. baking dish. Bake at 350° for 6–8 minutes or until golden brown; cool on a wire rack. In a mixing bowl, beat cream cheese and confectioners' sugar; fold in 1 cup whipped topping. Spread over cooled crust. In another mixing bowl, beat milk and pudding mix on low speed for 2 minutes or until thickened. Spread over cream cheese layer. Top with remaining whipped topping; sprinkle with cookie pieces. Refrigerate for at least 1 hour before serving. **Yield:** 12–15 servings.

Make-Ahead Shortcake

From Gove, Kansas, Karen Bland shares the recipe for this lovely layered dessert that showcases strawberries. "This family favorite has all the satisfaction of traditional straw-berry shortcake with just a dash of distinc-tion," she promises.

1 loaf (14 ounces) angel food cake, cut into 1-inch slices
½ cup cold milk
1 package (5.1 ounces) instant vanilla pudding mix
1 pint vanilla ice cream, softened
1 package (6 ounces) strawberry gelatin
1 cup boiling water
2 packages (10 ounces *each*) frozen sweetened sliced strawberries
Sliced fresh strawberries, optional

Arrange cake slices in a single layer in an ungreased 13-in. × 9-in. × 2-in. dish. In a mixing bowl, beat milk and pudding mix for 2 minutes or until thickened; beat in ice cream. Pour over cake. Chill. In a bowl, dissolve gelatin in boiling water; stir in frozen strawberries. Chill until partially set. Spoon over pudding mixture. Chill until firm. Garnish with fresh strawberries if desired. **Yield:** 12 servings.

Mint Chocolate Chip Pie

"Your guests will be requesting the recipe after one bite of this fluffy and refreshing pie," promises Laurie Bourgeois of New Bedford, Massachusetts. "It doesn't take much time to prepare, yet it tastes as though you spent hours in the kitchen."

2 cups heavy whipping cream
2 tablespoons confectioners' sugar
2 cups cold milk
1½ teaspoons peppermint extract
5–6 drops green food coloring, optional
2 packages (3.4 ounces *each*) instant vanilla pudding mix
1 cup miniature semisweet chocolate chips
1 pastry shell (9 inches), baked

In a small mixing bowl, beat cream and sugar until soft peaks form. In a large mixing bowl, combine the milk, extract and food coloring if desired. Add pudding mixes; beat on low speed for 2 minutes or until thickened. Fold in cream mixture and chocolate chips. Pour into pastry shell. Refrigerate for 3 hours or until set. **Yield:** 6–8 servings.

Fruity Brownie Pizza

In Laverne, Oklahoma, Nancy Johnson starts with a basic brownie mix to create this luscious treat that's sure to impress company. "Sometimes I add mandarin oranges for even more color," Nancy notes.

1 package brownie mix (8-inch pan size)
1 package (8 ounces) cream cheese, softened
⅓ cup sugar
1 can (8 ounces) pineapple tidbits
1 small firm banana, sliced
1 medium kiwifruit, peeled and sliced
1 cup sliced fresh strawberries
¼ cup chopped pecans
1 square (1 ounce) semisweet chocolate
1 tablespoon butter

Prepare brownie mix according to package directions. Spread the batter into a greased 12-in. pizza pan. Bake at 375° for 15–20 minutes or until a toothpick inserted near the center comes out clean. Cool completely. In a mixing bowl, beat cream cheese and sugar until smooth. Spread over crust. Drain pineapple, reserving juice. Toss banana slices with juice; drain well. Arrange banana, kiwi, strawberries and pineapple over cream cheese layer; sprinkle with pecans. In a microwave, melt chocolate and butter; stir until smooth. Drizzle over fruit. Refrigerate for 1 hour. **Yield:** 12–14 servings.

Raspberry Pudding Parfaits

"These raspberry parfaits are fast and fuss-free," notes Ruth Andrewson of Peck, Idaho, *"because I make them with convenient instant pudding and whipped topping. They look pretty and taste fresh."*

2 cups cold milk
1 package (3.4 ounces) instant vanilla *or* French vanilla pudding mix
1 cup whipped topping
1 pint fresh raspberries

In a mixing bowl, beat milk and pudding mix on low speed for 2 minutes. Fold in 1 cup whipped topping. Spoon a third of the pudding into six parfait glasses. Set aside six raspberries for garnish; divide half of the remaining berries over pudding. Repeat layers. Top with remaining pudding and garnish with the reserved berries. **Yield:** 6 servings.

Chilly Peanut Butter Pie

"My daughter requested this cool and creamy dessert instead of cake for her birthday," explains Marietta Slater of Augusta, Kansas. *"This easy pie is so popular, it disappears in a hurry."*

1 carton (8 ounces) frozen whipped topping, thawed, *divided*
1 graham cracker crust (9 inches)
½ cup strawberry jelly or jam
1 cup cold milk
1 package (3.4 ounces) instant vanilla pudding mix
½ cup peanut butter

Spread 1 cup whipped topping over the bottom of the crust. Drop jelly by tablespoonfuls onto topping; spread carefully. In a bowl, whisk milk and pudding mix until thickened. Add peanut butter; mix well. Fold in the remaining whipped topping. Spread over jelly. Cover and freeze for 4 hours or until firm. Remove from the freezer 10 minutes before serving. **Yield:** 6–8 servings.

Strawberry Slush

"This make-ahead slush is really refreshing on hot summer days," says Patricia Schroedl of Jefferson, Wisconsin. *"Pour lemon-lime soda over scoops of the strawberry blend for a fast fruity treat that's so thick you'll have to eat it with a spoon."*

1 quart fresh strawberries
2 cups nonfat vanilla ice cream, softened
1 package (.3 ounce) sugar-free strawberry gelatin
½ cup boiling water
2 teaspoons lemon juice
2 liters diet lemon-lime soda, chilled
Additional fresh strawberries, optional

In a large bowl, mash strawberries; add ice cream. In a small bowl, dissolve gelatin in water; stir in lemon juice. Add to the strawberry mixture; mix well. Pour into a 1½-qt. freezer container; cover and freeze overnight. Remove from the freezer 15 minutes before serving. Spoon into glasses; add soda. Garnish with strawberries if desired. **Yield:** 10 servings.

Chocolate Mallow Pie

"This rich and creamy dessert is so easy to assemble," assures Glenda Parsonage of Maple Creek, Saskatchewan. *"To save time, I often prepare and freeze a graham cracker pie crust so all I have to do is thaw it and then fill it."*

1 package (8 ounces) cream cheese, softened
2 cups cold milk, *divided*
1 package (3.9 ounces) instant chocolate pudding mix
1½ cups miniature marshmallows
1 graham cracker crust (9 inches)

In a mixing bowl, beat cream cheese and ½ cup milk until smooth. Add pudding mix and remaining milk; mix well. Fold in the marshmallows. Pour into the crust. Refrigerate until serving. **Yield:** 6–8 servings.

White Chocolate Tarts

"These are scrumptious but really no fuss, because they call for prepared tart shells, instant pudding and whipped topping," notes Traci Maloney of Toms River, New Jersey.

1 can (14 ounces) sweetened condensed milk
1 cup cold water
1 package (3.4 ounces) instant white chocolate pudding mix
2 cups whipped topping
2 packages (6 count *each*) individual graham cracker tart shells

In a mixing bowl, combine milk, water and pudding mix. Beat on low speed for 2 minutes. Cover and refrigerate for 10 minutes. Fold in whipped topping. Spoon about ⅓ cup into each tart shell. Refrigerate until serving. **Yield:** 12 servings.

Cherry Almond Tart

Connie Raterink uses on-hand ingredients, including canned pie filling and a cake mix, to create this dazzling dessert. "It's fast to fix, looks elegant and tastes delicious," says the Caledonia, Michigan cook.

1 package (18¼ ounces) yellow cake mix
⅔ cup graham cracker crumbs (about 11 squares)
½ cup butter, softened
1 egg
½ cup chopped almonds
1 package (8 ounces) cream cheese, softened
¼ cup confectioners' sugar
1 can (21 ounces) cherry pie filling
½ cup sliced almonds, toasted

In a mixing bowl, combine the cake mix, cracker crumbs and butter until crumbly. Add egg; mix well. Stir in the chopped almonds. Press onto the bottom and up the sides of a greased 14-in. pizza pan. Bake at 350° for 11–13 minutes or until lightly browned. Cool completely. In a mixing bowl, beat cream cheese and sugar. Spread over crust. Top with pie filling. Sprinkle with sliced almonds. Store leftovers in the refrigerator. **Yield:** 14–16 servings.

Dirt Pudding Cups

"These darling little desserts are my daughter Crystal's favorite," relates Linda Emery of Tuckerman, Arkansas. *"At birthday parties, the children love the individual servings because each gets a gummy worm."*

2 cups cold fat-free milk
1 package (1.4 ounces) sugar-free instant chocolate pudding mix
1 carton (8 ounces) reduced-fat whipped topping
1 package (16 ounces) reduced-fat chocolate cream-filled sandwich cookies, crushed
Gummy worms, optional

In a bowl, whisk milk and pudding mix for 2 minutes. Fold in whipped topping. Divide a third of the cookie crumbs and half of the pudding mixture among 10 dessert cups; repeat layers. Top with remaining crumbs. Garnish with gummy worms if desired. **Yield:** 10 servings.

Fruity Coconut Chocolate Trifle

"This luscious dessert will wow everyone who sees it, let alone tries it," promises Donna Cline of Pensacola, Florida. *Apricot preserves add a fruity touch to the pleasing pairing of chocolate and toasted coconut in this easy-to-assemble trifle.*

1 loaf (10¾ ounces) frozen pound cake, thawed
⅓ cup apricot preserves
⅓ cup plus 2 tablespoons orange juice, *divided*
1 package (4 ounces) German sweet chocolate
1¼ cups flaked coconut, toasted, *divided*
1¾ cups cold milk
1 cup half-and-half cream
1 package (5.9 ounces) instant chocolate pudding mix

Trim crust from top, sides and bottom of cake. Cut cake into 16 slices. Spread preserves over eight slices; top with remaining cake. Cut into 1-in. cubes. Place in a 2-qt. serving bowl; drizzle with ⅓ cup orange juice. Chop chocolate; set aside 2 tablespoons for garnish. Sprinkle remaining chocolate and 1 cup coconut over cake. In a mixing bowl, combine milk, cream, pudding mix and remaining orange juice; beat on low for 2 minutes. Spoon over cake. Sprinkle with remaining coconut and reserved chocolate. Refrigerate for at least 4 hours before serving. **Yield:** 10–14 servings.

Chocolate Raspberry Torte

"When our daughter requested this fancy layered cake for her birthday, I was afraid it would be difficult to make," recalls Rosemary Ford Vinson of El Cajon, California. "But it's so easy! Everyone oohs and aahs at how pretty it is."

1 package (18¼ ounces) chocolate cake mix
1 package (3 ounces) cream cheese, softened
¾ cup cold milk
1 package (3.4 ounces) instant vanilla pudding mix
1 carton (8 ounces) frozen whipped topping, thawed
2 cups fresh raspberries
Confectioners' sugar
Fresh mint and additional raspberries, optional

Prepare the cake according to package directions, using three greased and floured 9-in. round baking pans. Bake at 350° for 25–30 minutes or until a toothpick inserted near the center comes out clean. Cool for 10 minutes; remove from pans to wire racks to cool completely. In a mixing bowl, beat cream cheese until fluffy. Combine milk and pudding mix; add to cream cheese and mix well. Fold in whipped topping and raspberries. Place one cake layer on a serving plate. Spread with half of the filling. Repeat layers. Top with remaining cake; dust with confectioners' sugar. Garnish with mint and raspberries if desired. Store in the refrigerator. **Yield:** 12 servings.

Fruity Tapioca

Folks who like tapioca will enjoy this fruity variation from Louise Martin of Denver, Pennsylvania. Convenient canned peaches and mandarin oranges give refreshing flavor to an old standby.

4 cups water
1 cup sugar
⅓ cup quick-cooking tapioca
1 can (6 ounces) frozen orange juice concentrate, thawed
1 can (29 ounces) sliced peaches, drained and diced
1 can (11 ounces) mandarin oranges, drained

In a saucepan, combine the water, sugar and tapioca; let stand for 5 minutes. Bring to a full rolling boil. Remove from the heat; stir in orange juice concentrate. Cool for 20 minutes. Stir in the peaches and oranges. Transfer to a serving bowl. Refrigerate until serving. **Yield:** 10 servings.

Strawberry Cheesecake Pie

"This creamy concoction is so refreshing on a hot day and is also really easy to assemble," comments Janis Plourde from Smooth Rock Falls, Ontario. *With its appealing look, company will never know how simple it is.*

2 cups sliced fresh strawberries
¼ cup chopped almonds, toasted
1 tablespoon sugar
1 graham cracker crust (9 inches)
1 package (8 ounces) cream cheese, softened
2 cups cold milk, *divided*
1 package (3.4 ounces) instant vanilla pudding mix

In a bowl, combine the strawberries, almonds and sugar. Pour into crust. In a mixing bowl, beat cream cheese until smooth; gradually add ½ cup of milk. Add pudding mix and remaining milk. Beat for 1 minute or until blended; pour over strawberries. Cover and refrigerate for 2 hours or until set. **Yield:** 8 servings.

Mocha Angel Food Torte

Chocolate, toffee and a hint of coffee make this torte a popular request at Hillary Brunn's house. The Santa Rosa, California cook uses a few instant ingredients to give prepared angel food cake heavenly homespun flair.

1⅓ **cups cold milk**
  1 **package (3.9 ounces) instant chocolate pudding mix**
  1 **tablespoon instant coffee granules**
  1 **cup heavy whipping cream, whipped, *divided***
  1 **prepared angel food cake (10 inches)**
  2 **Heath candy bars (1.4 ounces *each*), crushed**

In a mixing bowl, combine milk, pudding mix and coffee; beat on low speed for 2 minutes or until thickened. Fold in half of the whipped cream. Cut cake in half horizontally; place the bottom layer on a serving plate. Spread with half of the pudding mixture. Top with remaining cake. Fold remaining whipped cream into remaining pudding mixture; spread over top and sides of cake. Sprinkle with crushed candy bars. Chill for 2 hours before serving. **Yield:** 10–12 servings.

Easy Strawberry Napoleon

"This rich pudding-like dessert is one of my family's absolute favorites," declares Karen Sawatsky of Vineland, Ontario. Fresh strawberries make a pretty topping while convenient saltine crackers form a no-fuss crust.

2 cups cold milk
1 package (3.4 ounces) **instant vanilla pudding mix**
1 cup heavy whipping cream, whipped
36 saltines
1 pint fresh strawberries, sliced

In a mixing bowl, beat milk and pudding mix on low speed for 2 minutes. Fold in the whipped cream. Place a third of the crackers in an ungreased 8-in. square dish (break crackers to completely cover bottom of dish). Top with a third of the pudding mixture. Repeat the layers twice. Cover and refrigerate for at least 6 hours. Top with strawberries just before serving. **Yield:** 9–12 servings.

Ladyfinger Cheesecake

Raspberry or cherry pie filling gives a festive appearance to this rich no-bake cheesecake. "This elegant-looking dessert makes a dramatic presentation," says Irene Pitzer of Nashville, Tennessee.

2 packages (11.1 ounces *each*) no-bake cheesecake mix
⅔ cup butter, melted
¼ cup sugar
1 package (3 ounces) ladyfingers (25 cookies)
1 package (8 ounces) cream cheese, softened
3 cups cold milk, *divided*
1 carton (12 ounces) frozen whipped topping, thawed
1 can (21 ounces) raspberry pie filling *or* flavor of your choice

In a bowl, combine contents of crust mix packages, butter and sugar. Press onto the bottom of an ungreased 10-in. springform pan. Arrange ladyfingers around edge of pan.

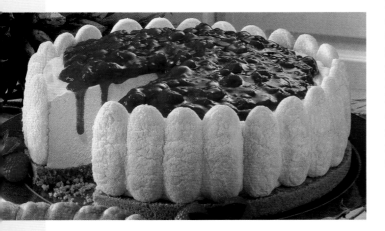

In a mixing bowl, beat cream cheese and ½ cup milk until smooth. Gradually beat in remaining milk. Add contents of filling mix packages; beat until smooth. Beat on medium for 3 minutes. Fold in whipped topping. Pour over crust. Cover and refrigerate for at least 1 hour. Top with pie filling. Remove sides of pan before serving. **Yield:** 12 servings.

Watermelon Gelatin Cups

Let these delightful watermelon wannabes from the Taste of Home Test Kitchen add a bit of fun to your next picnic spread. Limes are halved and hollowed to hold pretty pink gelatin while mini chocolate chips serve as seeds.

1 package (3 ounces) watermelon gelatin
1 cup boiling water
1 cup cold water
4 large limes
¼ cup miniature chocolate chips

In a bowl, dissolve gelatin in boiling water. Stir in cold water. Refrigerate for 1 hour or until slightly thickened. Meanwhile, slice limes in half lengthwise. With a small scissors or sharp knife, cut the membrane at each end to loosen pulp from shell. Using fingertips, pull membrane and pulp away from shell (discard pulp or save for another use). Fold chocolate chips into gelatin; spoon into lime shells. Refrigerate for 2 hours or until completely set. **Yield:** 8 servings.

Cinnamon Peach Cobbler

Prepared biscuit mix makes this comforting cobbler a quick favorite. "My husband loves the warm peaches, cinnamony sauce and golden crumb topping," notes Victoria Lowe of Lititz, Pennsylvania.

4 cups sliced peeled fresh *or* frozen unsweetened peaches, thawed
½ cup sugar
1 tablespoon plus ⅔ cup biscuit/baking mix, *divided*
½ teaspoon ground cinnamon
2–3 tablespoons brown sugar
¼ cup cold butter
3 tablespoons milk

In a bowl, combine peaches, sugar, 1 tablespoon of biscuit mix and cinnamon. Transfer to a greased, shallow 1½-qt. baking dish. In a bowl, combine the brown sugar and remaining biscuit mix. Cut in butter until crumbly. Stir in milk just until blended. Drop by rounded tablespoonfuls onto peach mixture. Bake at 400° for 20–25 minutes or until top is golden brown and filling is bubbly. **Yield:** 6–8 servings.

Streusel Strawberry Pizza

*"This is the best dessert pizza I've ever tasted,"
relates Karen Ann Bland from Gove, Kansas. The fruity treat is easy to put together, too, because it uses convenient cake mix and any flavor of canned pie filling. "It's great for children's parties," she adds.*

1 package (18¼ ounces) white cake mix
1¼ cups quick-cooking oats
⅓ cup butter, softened
1 egg
1 can (21 ounces) strawberry pie filling *or* flavor of your choice
½ cup chopped nuts
¼ cup packed brown sugar
⅛ teaspoon ground cinnamon

In a mixing bowl, combine the cake mix, oats and butter until blended; set aside ¾ cup for topping. Add egg to the remaining crumb mixture and mix well. Press into a greased 12-in. pizza pan. Build up edges and flute if desired. Bake at 350° for 12 minutes. Spread pie filling over crust to within 1 in. of edges. Combine the nuts, brown sugar, cinnamon and reserved crumb mixture; sprinkle over filling. Bake for 15–20 minutes or until lightly browned. Cool on a wire rack. Refrigerate any leftovers.
Yield: 8–10 servings.

Light Berry Mousse

"Members of my family are diabetic, so I'm always looking for sugar-free recipes," notes Peggy Key of Grant, Alabama. *"This light, fluffy dessert flavored with fresh strawberries is a refreshing ending to a summer meal."*

¾ cup boiling water
1 package (.3 ounce) sugar-free strawberry gelatin
1 cup ice cubes
1½ cups sliced fresh strawberries
¾ cup reduced-fat whipped topping

In a blender, combine water and gelatin. Cover and process until gelatin is dissolved. Blend in ice cubes until partially melted. Add strawberries; process well. Pour into a bowl; fold in whipped topping. Chill for 2 hours. **Yield:** 4 servings.

Banana Cream Dessert

"I entertain often, so this crowd-pleasing dessert is frequently on the menu," relates Evelyn Schmidt of Toms River, New Jersey. *"When cleaning up the dishes, there's never a crumb left to scrape off."*

3 cups graham cracker crumbs (about 48 squares)
½ cup butter, melted
3½ cups cold milk
2 packages (3.4 ounces *each*) instant vanilla pudding mix
5 medium firm bananas, halved lengthwise and cut into ½-inch slices
1 can (20 ounces) crushed pineapple, drained
1 carton (20 ounces) frozen whipped topping, thawed
⅓ cup chopped pecans, optional
2 milk chocolate candy bars (1.55 ounces *each*), broken into squares
Maraschino cherries, optional

Combine cracker crumbs and butter. Press into an ungreased 13-in. × 9-in. × 2-in. dish. In a mixing bowl, beat milk and pudding mix on low speed for 2 minutes. Pour over crust; top with bananas and pineapple. Spread with whipped topping (dish will be full). Sprinkle with pecans if desired. Chill for at least 4 hours before cutting. Garnish with candy bar pieces and cherries if desired. **Yield:** 16–20 servings.

Chocolate Pudding Pizza

"My sister Brenda and I made up this recipe while talking on the phone," explains LaDonna Reed of Ponca City, Oklahoma. *"My family loved the classic pairing of chocolate and peanut butter presented in a whole new way."*

1 package (17½ ounces) peanut butter cookie mix
1 carton (12 ounces) softened cream cheese
1¾ cups cold milk
1 package (3.9 ounces) instant chocolate pudding mix
1 carton (8 ounces) frozen whipped topping, thawed
¼ cup miniature semisweet chocolate chips

Prepare cookie mix dough according to package directions. Press into a greased 12-in. pizza pan. Bake at 375° for 15 minutes or until set; cool. In a mixing bowl, beat cream cheese until smooth. Spread over crust. In another mixing bowl, beat milk and pudding mix on medium speed for 2 minutes. Spread over the cream cheese layer. Refrigerate for 20 minutes or until set. Spread with whipped topping. Sprinkle with chips. Chill for 1–2 hours. **Yield:** 12 servings.

Apricot Angel Dessert

In Vulcan, Michigan, Beverly King tops cubes of fluffy angel food cake with canned apricot halves and a yummy sauce. "This light dessert is particularly good after a heavy meal," she says.

1 loaf (14 ounces) angel food cake, cubed
    (about 8 cups)
1 can (15¼ ounces) apricot halves, drained and diced
Sugar substitute equivalent to ½ cup sugar
3 tablespoons cornstarch
3 cups apricot nectar
1 package (.3 ounce) sugar-free orange gelatin
1 carton (8 ounces) reduced-fat frozen whipped
    topping, thawed

Place the cake cubes in an ungreased 13-in. × 9-in. × 2-in. dish; top with apricots. In a saucepan, combine the sugar substitute, cornstarch and apricot nectar until smooth. Bring to a boil; cook and stir for 2 minutes or until thickened. Remove from the heat. Stir in gelatin until dissolved. Pour over cake and apricots. Cover and chill for 3 hours or until gelatin is set. Spread with whipped topping. Refrigerate leftovers. **Yield:** 12 servings.

INDEX